To Bob

Son & Father

With love

[signature]

In My Father's Steps

In My Father's Steps

Don Tapping
Mark Tapping
William J. Turner

Dedicated to Theodore Hawley Tapping, Jr., whose inspiration and lessons encouraged this book to be written. It is further dedicated to all fathers and sons, so they too may cherish their relationships.

MCS Media, Inc.
All rights reserved.

Library of Congress Cataloging-in-Publication Data

Tapping, Don.
Tapping, Mark.
Turner, William.

In My Father's Steps

ISBN 0-9725728-6-4

Printed in the United States of America

We wish to acknowledge the following fathers and sons who shared their stories.

With deep appreciation to:

James and Rusty Ballas

Tom and Pete Franklin

Brian and Sye Hickey

Doug and Roger Kremer

Ron and Ronnie Landfair

Dennis and Ryan McDonald

Brian and Stu Tubbs

Biff and John Weber

Clayton and Tim Wilson

Table of Contents

Donkeys in the Derby

Fathers and Sons are a mysterious breed. The communication between them can be different than the communication between mothers and sons. Their relationship could be akin to donkeys trying to run in the Derby! It can be clumsy, but they seem to run the race all the same! This father and son are connected by a shared activity. For the father, the race had been run over and over. His son's race was just beginning, and it is here that they learn and connect. Their experience is one of actions rather than words.

The Father
In the blink of an eye...

October 31, 1988, Halloween, one of the best days for being with my sons, consisted in visiting houses and seeing them gather as much candy as they could. I found out that many adults were starting to give more healthy treats like granola bars, sugarless gum, animal crackers, and small juice packets. Parents would appreciate that, but the recipients, on the other hand, were a bit disappointed.

I had finished work early that day, around 4:00 PM, so I could rush home, get my running clothes on, and hit the trails. Running had been my escape the last few years from my work schedule. Running gave me at least an hour of time a day of total control. No matter whatever happened, I would get my run in. I enjoyed the days with the worst weather, as I felt I had even defeated the elements in their attempts to keep me inside. My work necessitated travel all over the world, usually one or two weeks per month. I would have preferred not to leave my three boys and my wife. She already worked away from home three days a week. The guilt was with me, but this was an important aspect of providing for my family. My wife never complained as I spoke to her from those business trips, but I could understand the difficulties she experienced as she prepared the children for school, handled the sick days, cleaned and did the laundry. The frustration for me was released a bit while I ran, probably much faster than I had ever run before. My four years Marine Corps trained me well in athletic endeavor. Those were mandatory runs, here I ran for a passion.

At the end of my run that afternoon, one of my younger sons said:" Let's go dad. How do you like my costume?"

"Great," I said, "I think this is your best year ever, dressing up like a football player. Tell Mom I will be ready in 10 minutes. I will take a quick shower and meet you and your brothers outside."

After I showered, we headed out to Grandma and Grandpa's house. The drive was about fifteen minutes. As we arrived I reminisced about all the years we have been coming here with the family. It had been about twelve years since my oldest was one year old. I remember that he had dressed like a pumpkin. The houses in the subdivision were closer together than our neighborhood, which meant more candy in less time! This yearly ritual brought enormous pleasure to my parents. Grandpa and Grandma always kept a few cans of apple juice in the refrigerator. Each little container fitted perfectly into our son's tiny hands and they delighted in pulling off the tab on their own. It made them feel grown up. They were hardly out of the car and inside the house before they were "thirsty."

That evening as they peered inside the refrigerator, they stared in horror at the empty shelves. No cans of apple juice. Grandma and Grandpa had forgotten about their special treat! The boys were already quite rambunctious; running around and screaming, and now their wails of disappointment were added to the confusion.

"I'll go to the store to get some," I suggested quickly to appease the boys and to escape the bedlam. "Dad, do you want to come with me?"

My father and I got in the car and chatted on the way to the local store. After purchasing the cans of apple juice, we rode back, exchanging pleasantries. As we approached the big oak tree on their street, gripping the steering wheel hard, I let it all out. "Dad, I'm so exhausted and stressed I can't even think. Kathy is tired too. We have not had a good night's sleep since the boys were born and not a single moment of tranquility. Sometimes I wonder if these constant physical demands will ever end. Do not misunderstand me, I want peace and quiet, but with my sons, not without them. When will they grow up?"

Dad turned to me, and putting a meaningful hand on my arm, said, "In the blink of an eye. You know, time will go by like the blink of an eye." A wistful look appeared on his face as he spoke, the kind of look mature men have when they visit their past and wish for some opportunity to take it on a different course; to be young again to relive one's life with the wisdom of old age and make each second count.

I was unaccustomed to my father sharing his inner thoughts. He had been a school principal all of his working life and ruled over students and teachers with an iron rod. He enforced the same stern discipline at home and would not tolerate misbehavior. For me there was no escape from his authority. I attended every school he directed from elementary to high school and, as the son of the principal, I had, at least in my mind, the daunting duty of living up to his and the school's expectation of me. That relationship did not encourage personal conversation. He was the head of my family, but I did not really know him.

His thoughts, hobbies and inner feelings were a mystery to me.

So, back in 1988, as my father said, "in the blink of an eye," with such feeling in his face and voice, I automatically glanced at the front dash digital clock of my car. It read 5:58 PM. Was it a reflex or deep inside me? Did I anticipate the future impact of his words on my life? The only thing I know for sure is that in that one moment something special passed between us. My father was sharing an intimate part of himself with me, a part I had never seen. It was a revealing, deepening experience. In his eyes I could read words he did not say: "Enjoy life, appreciate every moment of it, be positive, and do not yearn for the future at the expense of the present. Enjoy the race!" Many people had said the same thing to me, but his words, being out of character, meant more to me.

That day I concentrated more on this precious opening of his soul than on the potential influence of his words on my life. I did not yet have the age or the experience to appreciate the value of his lesson. In any case I was too busy raising three children and working two jobs to delve deeply into my thoughts. But every year, his words came back to me at random, at birthdays and holidays, causing me to reflect upon our special moment.

Some years later I realized the true meaning of my father's lesson. My wife and I finally had some peace, this time with our sons, all of us being a little older. They were, rightly so, pursuing their own interests. I suddenly thought, "Give me back my five and two-year olds! I know I can be different this time around. I've discovered what really matters to me. It's not sleep or peace, it's my sons. I want a chance to go back and have more patience, travel less and be more available."

I did not get the chance to relive the past, but from that

day onward I began to concentrate on the present and enjoy the race. I stopped traveling because I could not leave my family behind any more. Sons need us at any age.

There is not a day that I do not think of my father's words, as I drive up his street for those family birthdays and those Christmas holidays. I pass by the big oak tree which is still standing there. I wonder if someday it will come down with a strong wind or a winter snow storm. No, I do not think so. A calming feeling penetrates me. I am grateful to my father for making me think of what is important in my life. Time goes by like the blink of an eye. Do not squander any of it.

The Son
I raced with my dad...

One Saturday morning, when I was about ten, I was sprawled in my pajamas on the family room sofa watching my favorite cartoons. My dad popped his head inside the room and said, "I'm going for my run, do you want to come?"

It was a gray, damp, October day, the type that makes you want to snuggle under a warm blanket and watch the world go by. My dad had just returned home the day before from a two week business trip. I hesitated, torn between the TV and accepting his invitation.

It seemed like my parents had dragged me along since birth to my father's races, distances from 10K to marathons. He trained relentlessly for these events. No matter how tired he was, he was out there running on a nearby trail every night after work and on Saturdays and Sundays. At the races, Dad arrived at the finish line sweaty and exhausted and, watching him gasp for breath, I used to wonder why he would put himself through such pain. It seemed to me that nothing could beat the pleasure of a good cartoon. Maybe it was a manhood thing.

When he asked me that Saturday to go with him, I was torn between taking part in this manly ritual and discovering at last the great mystery behind running, and what this might cost me: loss of TV and probable intense physical pain. Ah, but there was my chance of impressing and getting closer to my dad. I glanced mournfully at the screen and switched the TV off.

"Ok," I heard myself say.

"Get dressed, put your sneakers on and let's go," he responded.

We jumped inside the car and drove to his usual trail. On the way there, I asked, "Dad, why do you run, it seems so painful?"

"It keeps me in shape physically and mentally. I sweat out stress and anxiety. I think clearer when I'm on the trail. It brings me peace."

"Why?' I said.

"Running allows me to control most things. It's almost most enjoyable when the weather is bad. You just got to do it and get it over with. It's so different from the office, it refreshes me."

"But, you always look in pain!"

He smiled. "That's part of the deal. Running pushes me beyond my limits. Beyond the pain, there is elation, a tremendous sense of achievement. After our run, you'll see what I mean."

We got out of the car. A penetrating dampness made me shiver with cold. A fleeting moment of regret for not being in warm pajamas overcame me.

"You need to stretch to loosen your muscles; otherwise you'll get hurt," Dad said as he showed me a few exercises.

"Ready?"

I nodded.

"Let's go."

We began the run. I kept up with him for a few yards, but my legs were too short and my lungs were out of training. Soon I dropped behind. Dismayed, I watched him take off. He ran further still. Meanwhile, I was battling cramps and a strong desire to go back to the car. Suddenly he turned around and ran back to me. We continued and he adjusted his pace to mine.

"Good job. Keep this pace up; it's a good one for you. I'll go off for a few minutes and come back."

Good job? Was I really doing a good job? His encouragement gave me some strength. I managed to keep on running. He ran ahead and came back to check on me at regular intervals. He probably covered eight miles to my four. But on this trail, a new one for me, it was comforting to know every few minutes he would be there like clockwork.

In spite of the burning in my chest and the cramps in my legs, my dad's words urged me on. "Come on, don't give up. Keep running, one step at a time. Don't focus on how far you still have to go, just keep your head down and focus on that next step. Remember Aesop's fable of the hare and the tortoise? They were in a race. Sure of winning, the hare hopped all over the place and the tortoise, aware of her shortcomings, plodded on and on, and won the race. That's what running does to you, gives you the will to get there."

What my Dad said made little sense at the time, but somehow stuck in my mind on that day and on that run. Determined not to disappoint him, I was able to go further than I thought was possible.

"Here was the rise that people refer to as Cardiac Hill," he said.

This was a hill about a quarter mile long, with a 45 degree incline, with rocks and trunks of trees fallen on the trail. Just when you think you arrive at the top, there is another 25 yards hidden around the corner.

'The last challenge! Let's meet it together!" He jogged by my side, coaxing me all the time.

"You can do it, you can do it. Come on, Son."

I was exhausted and in pain, but I never stopped running. Walking may have been faster, but I was not going to stop. I had to keep that jogging motion. It was a matter of pride and principle.

After we arrived at the first level, and then to the actual top, there was a downhill stretch which broke the uphill strain. My dad never told me about that, he wanted me to learn to keep going and take what comes to you. After about 5 more minutes I noticed we had circled back to near the beginning.

"Now, let's race to the finish," he said.

"And let me win!" I responded.

I jumped with joy and excitement. I had done it! "Dad, it was fun!"

That day I had lots of energy. I did not even switch the TV back on.

We ran together for four or five years and it was the best time of my childhood. By then I had caught up with him. We never talked while we ran. That first time we had said what needed to be said. The silent closeness we experienced was enough for later races. Words might have spoiled that.

We stopped running together when I went to high school. For some reason I had felt that was not really "cool" to do things with your parents at that age.

Now that I am in college, away from home, running is my daily ritual. It does give me the strength to go on, to tackle those tests, and other challenges. Running makes that easier. It may not be for the physical release of running, but more for the comfort that my dad is still with me on those runs. Every run, I remember that cool, gray, October morning and the right decision I had made. It was providential that my dad asked me, on that day and at that time.

He still talks about running around the lake at his college. I now run around that lake every day because I attend the same school as he did. As my feet pound the ground, I think of my dad and feel his support and encouragement. He is there, right by my side, coaxing me, "You can do it! You can do it," and pushing me harder and harder. I repeat it over and over in my mind, "I'll never give up! I'll keep my head down! I'll do the best I can!"

Dad's bad knees prevent him from running anymore. If we could run together again, this time I could be the one to come back to him and coax him up the hill. Even if he cannot be beside me now, I hope that one day a future run will be with a son of mine.

Capturing the Moment

Sometimes the big picture in life can overwhelm us. We can miss the forest for the trees. These two sons learned something valuable from their fathers as they focused on the more precious moments. A son's adolescent worries need the wisdom and assurance of a father who understands the dynamics and stress of new beginnings. With such support a son will find that an exciting adventure emerges.

The Father
For him it was an adventure...

"Do we all have to go?" I asked hoping my mother would simply cancel the whole trip.

"Yes, your Father looks forward to this trip all year and you know that it is always fun for us."

Usually I did not mind going, but I was now in high school. The same year after year family outing did not seem like it would be as much fun as Mom had thought. My parents and my brother and I traveled to Vermont every year during the summer to spend time with our family and to get away for a few weeks. In my younger years I really enjoyed the camping, hiking, fishing and the sports we played.

"Is everyone ready for a great trip?" My Dad enthusiastically asked us all, as if we were going on some kind of safari adventure.

"Yeah, Dad, I can't wait." I lied, just so I would not hurt his feelings.

My Father was a hard worker in all aspects of his life. He was extremely bright and for many years I thought he was the smartest man in the world. He just radiated wisdom. Whenever I had a problem, he always had something good to say that practically solved it. He was a psychologist and worked very hard to earn his numerous degrees. His studies occupied him constantly for some of the early years of my life. On his arrival home every night for the last few weeks, the first thing he would talk about would be our family vacation. Not only could he get away from his work, but he was able to spend some rare family time with the rest of us.

As the trip was underway I could not help but sit there in the car and think about how unhappy I was about being there. My brother was not very pleased either. In fact he was probably more upset than I was. I just could not see why Mom and Dad were unwilling go on this trip by themselves. We were old enough to stay home alone, and we had even stayed overnight at friends houses before.

"Oh, wow, look at that sight!" My dad yelled as he looked at what appeared to be a threatening rain cloud. We stopped the car and my father had to get out and take a picture. He loved photography, probably more than his work. If he was not doing anything work related and there was nothing else to do, I would find my father in the dark room in the basement. For years he had always had an obsession for taking pictures and developing them. I never realized why until I was much older and I understood my father and his habits.

He made us all get out of the car and focus on the picture he was about to take.

"What's so great about that?" I blurted out rudely.

"Do you see that amazing formation and the many different shades of gray?"

"I guess so, but it doesn't look that nice to me."

"This will look perfect once I get it developed."

Oh great, I thought, that means I will have to get another lecture about how to develop a picture in that dark room.

I felt that I had to pretend to be interested. He would often stop on the road whenever he would see something remotely interesting that he thought would be the "shot of a lifetime." I thought it was a waste of time, mostly because I just did not see what was so interesting.

After he had snapped a picture at every angle adjusting his camera he finally got back into the car. There were no words that could describe my dad after he had just taken a picture. He seemed as if he had just captured the meaning of life on film, and he appeared like this every time he took a picture of anything. Somehow my father really experienced something wonderful when he had his camera. Today, I simply could not explain my father's photographic obsession.

The trip was long and we amused ourselves by playing games. We had a sheet of items and whoever found those objects during the drive would be the winner.

"The sign!" I yelled hoping I would find something green.

"Nope." my brother added, knowing that I would never get it, "It was Mom's shirt."

We kept ourselves occupied playing 'I spy' games like this for most of the trip. In the 1960s we did not have a CD player or a portable video game machine. Many hours of driving passed listening to my parents talk about people they knew. Suddenly, Dad swerved the car, barely missing a vehicle that had cut us off.

"Dad, aren't you going to do something, he almost killed us!" my brother furiously reacted, as if he had personally been insulted.

"No, that's not how you should handle it. The man is probably in a hurry and needed to get by me, or he couldn't see me. He simply was going a bit too fast. We are all safe and that's all that matters. There is no need for retaliation for a little incident like this."

"Yeah, but he totally cut you off. I would have definitely let him have it. That guy wasn't in a rush, he was probably drunk."

It was true. The man was in an old beat up truck and was going very fast. He did not seem to really know what he was doing. This apparently drunk driver had practically killed us and my dad did not do anything about it but brush it off as if nothing had happened.

My mother was distraught, but we knew that she would not say anything to my father, at least not around us. They were very discreet in their relationship. They never fought in the home and rarely ever did I see my father express his love for my mother. They would occasionally kiss on the cheek, but rarely would I ever see them or hear them talk about a romantic type of love. My mother was a very happy woman who enjoyed playing the traditional role of a mother who stayed home to cook and clean. She worked hard for the family and my dad was always grateful and seemed to recognize all her hard work.

After this little incident was over we continued on an uneventful car ride towards the state of Vermont. It may have been a great state, but to me, this could mean a wasted week and a half. Throughout that ride I noticed myself paying more attention to my dad. I began wondering why he loved to stop and take so many pictures along the way and why he barely even recognized the fact that a drunk driver had almost killed us. He simply always saw that there was good in people.

Finally we arrived. We stayed at a summer cabin on a lake surrounded by pine trees. The water was clear and not a ripple could be found on a clear day. Even with all of the complaining I did in the car, I could not help but to take in the view and really appreciate being there. Surprisingly, I actually started to get excited about being there. Feelings of warmth and comfort began to fill me. It began to feel like such a secure place. It was no different than any year, but why was I so excited to be there?

"Everyone get your belongings and take them into the cabin," my dad ordered, as if we had just arrived at a military base.

When we entered the cabin I could not help but notice all of the writings we had carved in the wood over the years. We had always stayed in the same cabin and so many memories of those times rushed through my head. These trips were the highlight of my year when I was younger. I had totally forgotten why I did not want to be there. My brother, on the other hand, had not. He threw his bags on the bed, and walked out into the woods to be alone.

He had been in trouble recently, so he and my father were currently on bad terms. This was not unusual in their relationship. My brother had become an activist over the years and became very anti-government in his ideas. My father had always been a very political man and very supportive of government. My feelings were similar to my father, although not nearly as strong. There were many issues in the 1960s and my brother had become a poster child for teenagers of the age. Despite their differences my dad did not treat him any differently and let him have his space.

After we had settled and moved in, Dad and I decided to go fishing. It had been a few years since we were out on the lake and I was excited to spend some time with him. He had been working a regular eight hour day, and when he came home he went into his dark room and worked on his photos. There were not many hours left for us to spend together. Summer was the time when I was with him the most. Now that I am older, there seems to be even less time to enjoy each other's company.

As we headed for the lake I felt a little annoyed that again he had brought his camera along.

"Why do you have to take pictures of everything?" I asked him as soon as I saw the camera.

"I like capturing the moment. You never know if you'll ever see something like that again. If we didn't have pictures, we'd never be able to show anyone what we enjoyed."

That seemed wise enough. As he explained his feelings to me, I was beginning to understand him more and more. There was something special, something important, and something crucial about these pictures. I would continue to reflect on his hobby for years to come.

As we walked out onto the dock my dad turned to me.

"So how has school been lately?" he asked in his genuine voice.

"Good. We have a concert coming up."

"I know, I can't wait. I love to hear you play. Have you ever thought about taking that up as a career?"

"I don't know, I never thought of it," I responded honestly.

"Well you should, you are very good at it."

When my father talked like this, I was not very surprised. He was always encouraging my brother and I to do well. He continually praised everything we did. Whenever he supported me, it always put me in a better mood. Maybe it was this praise that set the trip off right. I was happy to be there after all! In fact, I probably would not have wanted to be any other place in the world!

We continued to fish and we had an excellent time. Our conversation consisted of how I did in school or how my music lessons were proceeding.

The whole family went fishing, hiked trails and ate dinner together every night. I do not remember any particular difference in activities in this year than in any other year. I do remember reflecting on my father and paying closer attention to him. He seemed so happy with whatever he did. There was not a care in the world for us as he tried to please everyone and make everyone happy. We had been together for nine days.

Our vacation passed by in a flash. Before I knew it we were on our way home and I was exhausted and I took the opportunity for a nap. Opening my eyes a few times, I noticed my dad. He seemed at complete peace with our family. Why was he so peaceful? This yearly ritual was no different than any other. Why was it so special to me? My father and I did not have very many long conversations, but we knew our love was there.

In the last few years of his life my father was not himself. Illness and old age prevented him from having his usual enthusiasm. But these last years are not what I remember. What I recall is a supportive man who constantly encouraged people to pursue their lives with enthusiasm. During his supportive moments he was able to show his love for me and his grandchildren.

As I look back on that one trip, I remember how many events brought out my father's strengths. The man who cut us off while we were in the car was a little incident but his reaction was a major theme in his life. He never acted with vengeance and had the ability to calm others. He was tolerant to my brother even though they disagreed on so many issues. He told my brother and I to work things out and that the use of violence does not solve anything. As I watched my children grow, I encourage them to communicate and I encourage them work out their problems. I have many opportunities to mentor children as I continue my teaching career.

My father loved to photograph everything. We now have many wonderful pictures of different sunsets and landmarks. Years ago I would not have looked twice at these pictures, but as I looked at them on the day of my father's funeral, I understood why he took them. He simply wanted to capture the moment. He wanted us to see everything he saw and share his outlook on life. I began to see that he was taking pictures of the good in everything. All his pictures were of people smiling, beautiful landscapes, and famous landmarks. There were no gloomy pictures. His wisdom remains for me now even after his death. He had helped me to understand his life.

I once thought that I had not learned a great deal from my father. I now realize that in our conversations about my life and in his supportive nature he helped me to understand people and to understand life. All of us can mentor without actually saying words. Today, I teach sixth and eighth graders and I continue to reflect upon my father's ways by striving to be just as supportive to them as he was to me. I continue to capture the moment as I share in the life journeys of my children.

The Son
You'll be fine...

My stomach was in knots and I was drenched in a cold sweat. I had been tossing and turning all night and could not fall asleep. Tomorrow marked my first day of high school. Most of us were probably quite nervous on our first day as well, but when you have attended a private school all of your life, and you have seen the same faces, switching schools is no easy task.

I had made many friends in private school and I did not want to leave. My dad was the headmaster there for years. He had taught my science class in the sixth and the eighth grade. I had seen my father at school my entire life, and now I had to go to a school where I would see hundreds of new faces, none of whom I could count on for support. It was a somewhat daunting feeling, even for a thirteen year old, knowing that my father would not be there, on site, if I needed him.

I finally fell asleep. My dreams that night were very bizarre. One of them consisted of me walking through school with my shirt off in a long cold corridor. When I awoke, a feeling of complete terror struck me. I realized the day was here. The shower was out of hot water so I had to take a short quick rinse. I did not feel very clean. This was not a good way to start the day.

"Are you ready for breakfast?" my mom called up the stairs as I readied myself.

"Yeah, I just have to dry off."

"She's making breakfast?" I thought as I began to put on my clothes. My mom rarely made breakfast. What was she preparing me for? The last time she made breakfast for me was when I went to my first major league baseball game and I was seven years old. I knew it was a special occasion, but knowing that only made me more nervous.

"This is a real good breakfast," I said as I forced it in my mouth knowing that if I ate it fast it might make me feel sick and that could be a good way out.

"Don't eat so fast, you don't want to get sick on your first day" she added as if she knew exactly what I was thinking. I never said anything at the breakfast table about how I felt. I am sure that they all knew my anxiety because I had whined about my apprehensions all summer. Most of my other friends were going to another high school, but my parents wanted me to attend a smaller one that was closer to home. I therefore decided to place the blame on my parents and, wise as they were, they probably knew that.

My father took me to school that morning, just as he had taken me for the eight previous years. He had notified his office that he would be a little late because he had something important to do. That something important was to be with me as I prepared to begin this first day at my new high school. I was more nervous this morning than I had been in years. Could it only get worse?

On the way, my dad and I talked our usual small talk. The weather outside was beautiful. It was a late summer day around 75 degrees with a steady breeze keeping it cool. The sky was completely clear and the sun was in our faces making it hard to see while driving. We talked about the Yankees and how they would make some trades in the off-season and get better. However, we quickly ended that conversation and shrugged our shoulders saying, "Whatever!" The conversation shifted to the weather, but never anything about the approaching ordeal. Dad never talked about things that would make either of us uncomfortable. He once told me that he would only make a comment when he knew that it was appropriate and necessary.

"By the way," he added, "I was hoping to pass Grandpa's camera on to you this year. Would you like to have it?"

"Gee, I don't know, Dad," I replied, "I'm not even sure I know how to use it."

"Well, we can talk about it later," he said. "It has really been an interesting hobby for me over all these years."

As he spoke we arrived in front of the school and I knew the time had come. Dad parked right next to the flagpole closest to the front door. I looked out the window to see a group of boys shoving each other and laughing. To the left of them were five girls gathered around in what looked

like a secret conversation. Everyone had someone, everyone but me. I was not in the mood for a pep talk at this
point, so I was glad to reach for the handle and say goodbye.

"Good luck, we'll see you when you get home."

"Thanks, Dad. See ya." I said as I walked away.

"Just a minute," my dad said in a stern yet caring voice
forcing me to turn around, "You'll be fine, Son."

That was all that he said; yet that prophecy was what I
was hoping would be the case. So I continued up the side-
walk towards that ominous building. As I walked through
the department store-like double doors, I was over-
whelmed by the crowd of teens who seemed to take note
of someone new. As I approached them, I felt as if everyone had stopped what they were doing to notice 'the new
kid'. This was going to be a very long day!

My first class began and it could not have been soon
enough. I felt as though I had been sitting alone at the table
for hours. The teachers were trying to make all this interesting, but some of the students were obnoxious, not listening to a word that was said. Three boys in the back tried
to talk to me, but I was afraid to join them for fear of making a bad impression with the teacher.

The rest of the day was much like the first hour. I sat
alone in all of my classes, imagining what it would be like
if I had friends around, and wishing the day would just be
over. Home was the only thing on my mind. Finally, the
last bell rang and it was time to go to soccer practice. I felt
that although it had been a terrible first day that I would
still be fine because at least I could make some friends on
the field.

I suited up and headed towards my first soccer practice.
Having already played for seven years, I felt I was a good
player and I would make a lot of friends because of that

experience. After the first few minutes, I realized that my hopes could not have been any further from the truth. No matter how good I thought I was at the game that did not seem to matter. Everyone else seemed to have their friends and nobody was about to talk to me. Every time I was open for a pass they would pass it to someone else or they would take it by themselves. These boys were not any different than the three boys in the back of class. Feelings of uneasiness began to settle in after practice because my intentions of making friends had not come true.

It had been exactly how I dreaded it would be; I was completely alone and not making new friends. All I could think about was how good it would feel when I got into the car with my dad. Even though he may have been wrong about today, I still wanted to simply be with someone I recognized. When I finally saw that brown Volvo it was the best sight of the day! When I got into the car he asked me how my day had been and simply gave him an "Ok." He obviously did not believe me.

"You'll be fine," he said out of nowhere. "It will all develop perfectly and you will have a great year in school. You just need to find those people who make you feel good."

"There's nobody, Dad, I looked, even at soccer nobody talked to me."

"Don't worry, you'll be fine."

I did not believe him anymore. How could he know? He has never had to go through anything like this. All of his life he had been at the same school and never had to move. It is easy for him to say because he rarely had to move from job to job in his life. We sat in silence. He had to know that I was upset.

At home, my mother wasn't much help either. I was not about to listen to her because it sounded like she had already planned a response with my dad. I stayed in my room that night. As I lay in bed I could not help but pray that tomorrow would be a better day.

I woke up the next morning with no better feelings. I had to ride the bus that day. It was not a great way to start the second worst day of my life. As I got on the bus, I soon realized that I was surrounded by a group of boys who appeared to be very unsocial, much like all of the others with whom I had come in contact the day before. As I sat there alone on the bus, I began to think of my dad's words: "You'll be fine, find somebody who makes you feel good." I began to think that I was bound to meet someone and have some friends. There has to be at least one person who would be willing. It is impossible to have a school of eleven hundred boys and none of them looking for a new friend. As I thought about this I began to see how my dad could say such a thing. He knew the odds were in my favor. There were so many students there that the chances are I would indeed find a friend! So although I had sat completely alone on the bus ride, I was in a more hopeful mood when I arrived at the school.

This day was much better from the very beginning. In each of my classes I was involved in the discussions which allowed most teachers to learn my name. At lunch I sat alone again. As boys walked by I would occasionally glance up and give somewhat of a welcoming smile hoping that they might sit down.

"Hey, what's up?" someone asked as he set his lunch tray down next to me.

"Hey, nothing much," I said, a little taken aback at the fact someone had finally spoken to me.

He was a pale, lanky lad who was taller than most freshmen. His radiant smile was very welcoming and was a sight for my eyes.

"You new here?" he genuinely asked as if he did not know.

"Yeah, I went to Emerson last year."

"Oh yeah, I just moved here from Maryland. You know anyone?"

"Nope," I said in almost an excited voice "Do you?"

"No man, yesterday was my first day. Soccer practice was rough yesterday, huh?"

Yes! He was just like me! Knowing that this might be my only chance to make a new friend, I encouraged the conversation.

"Yeah, it was rough. Hey you want to hang out this weekend?"

"Sure, there are good movies playing if you want to go catch one."

"Sounds good," he said.

We spent the entire weekend together. At night we stayed up late talking about sports and girls we saw at school. My new friend was in the same boat as me yet he struck me as somewhat shy. Was he as happy about our new found friendship? That Saturday night as we were lying on the couch I asked him about it.

"Hey, are you down for some reason?" I asked, hoping it was something he would talk about with me.

"I'm wondering about the other guys. I mean, we're having a great time together, but it just seems like we're isolating ourselves."

"Don't worry," I said reassuringly, "we'll be fine."
I could not believe the words that had come out of my mouth! Why would I say something like that? We had been at school an entire week and I had not even talked to anyone else other than this new friend. Then it flashed in my

mind. It was my father's car rides and his words of wisdom. It had worked out, just as he said it would.

As I lay in bed that night I was still somewhat anxious about my future in this new high school. Although there was now a person with whom I could share these feelings of doubt, even he felt that we were only two people among eleven hundred students.

That Monday at school was even better than the week before simply because I now had that connection I needed. The great part of that day was soccer practice. My new friend and I would work to become members of the team as well as friends. As we made good plays we exchanged special handshakes and nicknames.

"Nice pass, Scooter!" I'd say in a joking voice as I ran by, giving him a quick slap on his arm.

"Good finish, Dunker!" he said as I put the ball in the net.

The members of the team started to catch on and before we knew it we were all participating. They would run by each other making up new nicknames and new funny little handshakes to do. Before we had realized it, we were truly part of the team.

As I walked away from practice that day, a few boys came up to us and we decided that we would spend the weekend together. It had happened. By allowing my friend and I to just enjoy ourselves, and not worrying about making new friends, we had become an integral part the team and we had indeed made a great group of friends.

It had been one week since my disastrous first day of high school. I was sitting after practice talking to my friends and the brown Volvo pulled up with my dad in the driver's seat. This time I was not as anxious to get in and actually wanted to continue conversing with all of my new found friends. As Dad and I drove away from the fields, an extreme feeling of accomplishment filled me. I was on top of the world and could not have been any happier.

"Thanks, Dad," I said to him. He knew what I was talking about.

"I told you, Son, as long as you focus on the right things the picture will always turn out right."

When I got home I went up to my room and did a little thinking. As I reflected on my past week I realized that I had come a long way in developing friendships. I turned my head to my desk to see a picture of my Grandpa's face looking at me and I remembered what my dad had told me about Grandpa's camera. I hurried down the stairs to find him. He was reading the paper at the kitchen table and did not notice me until I said, "Dad, do you remember talking about Grandpa's camera?"

"Yes, the camera, but you didn't seem to want it."

"I do now. It just hit me why it's important and I see why my grandpa loved it so much."

Dad went into the closet and pulled out that old classic camera that my grandfather had used all his life. I had never even seen it before, yet it looked so familiar. It was bulky and black with buttons all over it. As I held it, I looked at my dad and smiled my thanks. To this day it sits in my room as a constant reminder of that experience and a symbol of how to get through the tough times in life.

My dad was right. He had helped me through this ordeal. Although our communication about our feelings and about our relationship was not a common occurrence, he still had a tremendous impact on my life and the decisions I have made since.

My father could not predict the future and he never actually knew exactly what was going to happen. He simply supported me so I could become successful. It was not until later that this realization came to me. If he had not been there telling me everything would be fine, I might not have built the confidence to find friends and succeed in my goals.

In reflecting on my father and his impact upon me, I see these experiences as moments where I was taught many life lessons. He allowed me to realize that people are generally good and that you need to focus on what is important to you. I found friends in high school, in college, and will continue to find meaningful relationships throughout my life. I will always hear my dad's words of wisdom. "Yes, I know I will be fine, Dad. I will focus on my shot, and on those little details. I know now that the big picture will turn out as well!"

My Father's Business

Fathers of the past have been in nine to five jobs earning a living for their families. The home and its events have sometimes taken a second position to the workplace. Does a son often learn lessons from the experience of his father's business away from home? It is wonderful to hear from these sons that they do not have memories of fathers who are absent from their lives as they labor in the workplace. They have been able to learn from "their father's business" that not only does he provide for them financially, but he will always love and support them.

The Father
Lessons at work...

The sun was hot and the car felt as if it were going to melt. It was a scorching 98 degrees and not a cloud in the sky. Everybody who was in their right mind was probably at the beach or on their way to it. I, on the other hand, was not thinking about the weather. Thirty minutes ago I had just received a phone call from my father from his house across town telling me my mother was ill.

As I sat in the L.A. traffic, I began to think about what my father said on the phone. "Your mother is sick and she needs you to look after her." My dad was heading on a trip to India for two months and he needed my help. He had important business there, and he was not about to miss it. He was such a proud person that he would never admit he needed help for anything. His method always consisted of asking other people to assist a third party. This time it was a serious situation.

Throughout my childhood my father was never late for

a single appointment. Ever since I can remember he had the same routine. He probably did not change his routine for any reason. Every morning he would wake up at the exact same time, shower at the same time and walk out the door to work at exactly 7:15. He would arrive home after work at 5:30, read the paper until 5:55, and dinner would start at 6:00. He would go into his bedroom at 10:00, read for fifteen minutes, and his light would shut off at 10:15. His life was like clockwork. There were no exceptions. Some of the worst stress I felt in high school was worrying about not being home in time for dinner because a coach would hold us too long at a practice.

Reflecting on these old memories of my father made the drive seem brief. As I pulled up to their home, I could not help but to feel a little uneasy about the situation. My mother had never been ill before and they had rarely ever asked me to help them. The feelings of uneasiness soon disappeared when I entered the house and saw my mother's smiling face.

"Oh, its good see you, Mom," I said, hugging her and ignoring the fact that I knew she was ill.

"You need to visit more. Where's Karen?" My mom quickly jumped to another subject so she would not have to talk about the situation.

"She's at home. The baby kept us up most of the night," I added. We had only been married a year and we had our first child a few months ago. I had been married previously and had children, but this felt different. Many people say the second time is better because you learn from your mistakes, and I was just beginning to believe it. Even my parents acted differently this time. I could tell by the way they were excited to see the family.

"Where's Dad?" I asked. I knew that he was getting ready to leave for his trip.

"He's in the bedroom packing."

My mother and I continued talking about the baby and other things that had been going on in our lives. We were still exchanging pleasantries when my dad walked in. We nodded, recognizing each other's presence. That is how we communicated. There was a shrug here, a nod there, and occasionally a few words thrown in. Even with the little verbal communication, this style suited us well. We never shared our emotions or even hinted that we had them. Although this worked for us, I always felt that deep down there were more things that could be said. I knew that with our stubbornness there probably never would be an outward display of emotions. He refrained from talking about the situation because he hated asking for help. I knew this, so nothing was said. He then turned to my mother.

"Do you need anything?" he asked.

"No Honey, I'm fine."

He turned to me: "Can you take me to the airport in an hour?"

"Yes, that would be fine," I said.

After this short appearance, my Dad walked into his office and shut the door. It was unlike him to miss the opportunity for work and he rarely ever worked out of his office. He needed to be home for my mother. My mother and I continued discussing what we would do in the next few weeks while my dad was away. We decided that I would take her to church, to the grocery store, and to the pharmacy to get her medicines.

Exactly an hour later my father left his office. I knew his pattern so I had already put on my shoes and was ready to leave. The car ride was not too long and the traffic had already subsided. He was meeting a business associate at the airport, so he was well dressed. His cuffs were a perfect length and his red tie looked more than suitable against his light blue shirt. There was not a flaw in his entire appearance. Every workday of my father's life he wore a perfectly pressed suit and always wanted to look like what he used to call "a million bucks."

As we drove in the car my dad made one reference to my mother's health.

"Don't worry, she'll be Ok. She just needs to rest."

The rest of the conversation was completely about my wife and our newborn. I knew there was more, I could tell. Why did my dad not want to open up? Maybe I should just initiate the conversation. I was, after all, forty years old. We arrived before I had found the courage to follow through with the plan. We pulled up to the short term parking lot and after a quick stop at the check-in desk we passed through security and were at the gate. It was thirty minutes before the flight was scheduled to board, yet there were travelers everywhere. People looked as if they were lining up just to sit down. Charles, one of his business partners, was already waiting for him in the hallway between terminals.

"Don't these people have lives?" I joked as I shook Charles' hand and looked at the crowds of people.

"I swear, every time I come here I have to practically sit on someone's lap to get a seat," he replied laughing.

My dad and he shook hands but they did not joke about the situation. For them it was all business. I sat there for a while talking with Charles about his wife and his kids. He then told me that they were still expecting someone from their company to bring samples that were needed for the trip. Soon, two men carrying those samples arrived and handed them to my father. His response was anger.

"What the hell is this?" he said as he looked at the samples in disgust.

"They are the samples you asked for," this middle- aged man said in a tiny little voice.

"No, these aren't the ones!" my dad yelled as he punted the samples several yards away.

I could not believe my eyes. My dad was making such a public scene for something that did not seem very important. It made me consider how difficult it would be to work for him.

I turned to Charles and asked, "Does he always do this?"

"Yeah," he said, "think nothing of it; he'll be calmed down in a minute."

And sure enough, it was true. The next thing I remember seeing was my dad shaking hands with the men and discussing what he needed. I did not understand my father. Apparently he acts like this often, but it is because he demands the same effort and efficiency that he gives to his company. I thought the reason for this outburst might have been because of my mother's illness. Perhaps my mother was more ill than I thought. Had my mother's illness affected him this much?

Before he got on the plane I shook his hand. He told me to take care of Mom, that she would be fine and that he hoped she would not need that much attention. This only made me more anxious about her condition. I knew he loved her and, for him, this was the closest thing to concern.

I stayed with my mother most of the time, occasionally going back and forth between my house and her house. I was able to see my new son almost every day. It was very important to me to be there for him.

Every Sunday I would take my mother to church which was another responsibility my father took seriously. I had never known him to miss church on Sundays. Each time I picked her up for the ride I could see her health diminishing. She was weaker and required more and more assistance even walking to the car.

My dad called every day to assure my mother that business was going well and she would always respond with an "I'm fine" or a "don't worry about me." I could see the fear in her eyes and heard the weakness in her voice when she talked to him. This was not an illness that could be brushed off. My dad needed to be home.

After six weeks of my mother struggling to go about her day to day activities, I decided it was time to call him. I left a message at the hotel where he was staying and I received a call back from him within the hour.

"What's the matter? Why are you calling me?" he snapped as soon as I picked up the phone.

"Mom's condition has really deteriorated," I said. "I think you need to come home."

"I'll be home in a few days." he said, never wanting to take advice from anyone.

"Dad," I said again," you need to come home now."

"Alright, I'll be home as soon as I can."

I could not believe it. As I listened to him on the phone I began wondering if he was in denial. Why would he not accept the fact that my mother was sick? It was the first time I ever stood up to my father. It may have been the best thing I had ever done.

It was a good thing he was coming home because of the doctor's latest prognosis. It indicated that my mother was dying. She was a strong woman who had provided for me and my dad throughout my life. She never missed making a dinner or going to my sporting events. Would Dad make it home in time?

Each day I sat in the hospital telling her he would be there soon. After three days he arrived and rushed in.

"How are you, Dear?' he asked my mom in an unusually loving way as he gave her a kiss on the cheek that seemed to release much of his anxiety.

As they hugged I saw my mother's hand grip my dad's back hard.

"I'm good," my mom lied, "how was your trip?"

"It was fine, I'm sorry I didn't come home sooner."

As I watched my mom and dad have this conversation I looked at my dad and saw a side of him I had never seen before. I knew that he cared about our family and loved us all very much. The caring in his eyes and the passion he expressed for Mom was deeper than I can relate. There was no more denial. He knew how sick she was and he showed her how much he cared.

My mother passed away two days later. The funeral was on a Saturday at 10:00 am at St. Michael Church, the same church where I had taken her every week. It was a closed casket; probably because my father wouldn't be able to handle it any other way. He and I were gracious to everyone and thanked everyone for coming, keeping our feelings inside as usual. My parents were loved by so many people and hundreds of people showed up for Mom's funeral. It was more difficult losing my mom, as I had no siblings with whom to share my grief.

After the funeral we had a few friends over to our house for a small brunch. Dad showed little emotion and appeared as if he had lost all sense of feeling. As I was ending a few conversations with the guests, I looked over and saw my dad staring out the window. I slowly approached him and I noticed as he peered out, that his jaw was clamped and his face stiffened. He was glaring out the window looking angrier than I have ever seen him. Those short weary gulps of breath were uncommon for his strong stature. I walked up to him and joined him looking out the window. It was then that he spoke the first words in private to me in three days.

"Damn it," he said with a long pause, "I'm going to miss her." He squeezed out the words between his teeth. A single tear rolled down his face onto his suit. It was the first tear I had ever seen him shed. The intensity in his face and the single tear demonstrated more emotion than I ever thought a person could show. That single tear had more love in it than a lifetime of others. I stood there with my arm around him, both of us looking out that window. There was never to be another moment that we would talk about my mother's death. As his son, I had expected him to show more love. In that single tear he had shown me how much he loved my mom and me. Dad and I had bonded.

I have learned from my father much about how important love is. He never showed love and I did not think he felt love. Although I never heard my father say the word, I now knew that love was there. He had tremendous love for our family and never showed it until I was forty years old. The memory of that one moment helps remind me never to miss those special events with my sons. I am committed to spreading my love over a lifetime to them. My father showed his love for others by being a man of strength and routine. I now have taken on that example of love and learning from my father and I hope that my sons will see that same loving strength in me.

The Son
My day in the workplace…

The time had finally arrived. I had looked forward to this day for so long. Today was 'take your son to work day.' I was sixteen, and for years I had visited my dad at work, but this time I would be able to spend an entire day with him and experience what his business was like.

From the moment I woke up I was so excited I could not wipe the smile off my face. I jumped out of bed and took a quick shower, making sure I was completely ready for my first business experience with my dad. The previous night I had already set out the clothes I was going to wear. As I put on my sweater and dress pants I looked in the mirror to see an ever so business like reflection. I began to wonder what sort of events would happen on this first day of work. Would I be able to sell a car to somebody? Will he let me test drive a car with someone? Maybe he will let me see one of those new cars in the back. The ideas were endless and I was so excited about just the thought of all the possible jobs I could be doing.

"How do I look, Dad?" I said as I was walking down the stairs to the kitchen.

"Good, you look really professional," he said with his warm, genuine smile.

For as long as I can remember my father has never said anything to me that made me feel embarrassed or hurt. He was the most loving father anyone could ask for. At home he was helpful around the house and joined in our play time. He was there for us even though he owned a car dealership and needed to be there quite often. Even when he was at work, he always made it clear that his office was always open for us to visit. I visited quite frequently, but today was different. Today I would get to spend the whole day and watch my dad in action. Would he act differently at work than he acted at home? Would he do business in front of me? Maybe I could make a sale by myself. As far as I was concerned, the possibilities were endless and the sky was the limit.

We sat down and ate breakfast with the family. The entire time I was smiling, glancing over at my dad. He probably knew how excited I was, but he did not say anything that would only overemphasize what for him was a regular workday.

"So what are we going to do today, Dad?" I asked. I was expecting to hear something completely out of the ordinary.

"Well, today I have a few meetings and I have some jobs for you."

He had some jobs for me! I couldn't believe it; he actually had things for me to do there. This was going to be the best day ever. Not only will I be able to watch my dad work, I'll be able to help him work.

At this point in my life I was completely set on the fact that I would one day take over the family business. Even at just eleven years old, I thought that I would play a crucial role in helping my dad out for the day. Although the events to come would not be considered exciting to most young people, to me they were the highlight of my childhood to this point.

We left the house at about eight o'clock on a cool, rainy day. It was quite windy and as the rain hit my face it made it seem much colder than it actually was. We left a little late, but it did not matter. My dad never followed a routine. His philosophy was when something needed to be done, he would do it, and it did not matter when or where. He hated routine and did whatever was necessary to get away from it. Although he would schedule some meetings, he still managed to go about his day in a somewhat unpredictable fashion.

As we pulled up to the dealership, an unshaven man who was covered in grease stepped out from the garage.

"Hello, Mr. Dornby, how are you today?" he eagerly asked.

"Not too bad, how are the young ones doing in baseball?" my dad replied in his ever so caring voice.

The thing about him was that he always seemed to care about every conversation and made each person know that he cared. He would always finish with a genuine "you take care of yourself, now" or a "well I really hope that goes well for you." The man left in high spirits despite his drenched jacket from the downpour of rain.

As we entered the building most everyone we walked past gave him a genuine greeting. We continued on our way past the employees and through the showroom. I could not help but to feel extremely proud to be his son as I walked next to him. You could tell by the expression on the faces of the employees that they were content with their job and with their employer. Looking back on it, I see how my dad was so successful. He created a working environment that people loved.

We turned the corner to see one of my favorite places in the world, my dad's office. It was like a second home to me. I would stop by and visit him at least once or twice a week. He always welcomed me and told me to come in and talk to him. There was always a golden glow radiating from the room. As I walked in, I took in the surroundings more than usual. I headed for the candy dish, which as always was full, and chose my favorite kind, one that would last a while. Dad told me to sit down while he took some phone calls and checked his messages.

While sitting in the old, green leather chair, in which I had sat so many times, I began to think about all the possible exciting jobs he had in store for me. I sat there patiently waiting for him to assign me the first of many. Between calls he turned to me and said, "Tom, could you please go ask Shelly at the front desk for a fax that was sent over for me?"

"Yeah, Dad, I'll get it right away," I said as I was already heading out the door.

My first real job! I hoped I would not make a mistake. As I rounded the corner I came face to face with a man who was carrying a briefcase. He was familiar and I felt that I had been introduced to him before. He recognized me as well and smiled his greeting.

"Hello there, is your dad around?"

"In his office," I responded as I focused on my mission continuing my walk down the hall.

I picked up the fax at the desk and I was excited to bring it to my dad. Just as I rounded the corner I saw that glowing, always welcoming office door was shut. I had never seen it shut before. As I was waiting for it to re-open I heard my dad from inside. He was obviously angry. This man who was visiting him must have brought him some disappointing news. As I listened, I realized that I had never heard my dad react like this before. He never swore, even at home, but here it seemed different. The door opened and the visitor came out giving me a smile and saying goodbye as if nothing had happened.

"Here you go, Dad," I managed to get out as I entered, not nearly as excited as I was before.

"Thanks, Tom," he said as I sat down on the chair.

"Dad, what was that all about?"

"Oh, you heard that?" he asked, knowing that it was impossible for me not to have heard. "I was just a little disappointed in the lack of effort with some people. If I work hard, I expect others to work hard as well. All I ask for is their honest effort. But don't worry, we have it all sorted out."

"Are they working hard now?" I asked, trying to be as involved in this situation as possible.

"Yes, we have everyone working hard now," my dad said with a little chuckle in his voice.

"Ok, are you ready to take a tour of the place?"

"Yes, but don't we need to do some work?" I asked a little confused.

"That can wait. Let's go show you the shop."

We proceeded out of his office to the giant garage that was next to the office building. As we walked in everyone gave a wave or a nice smile to my dad. He always replied with a friendly gesture or with a short conversation. You could see in his face how happy he was to be in his position as he interacted with each person. He was proud of his workers and enjoyed seeing them at their jobs. I did not realize any of this that day, but after I have reflected upon it for many years I now understand this is why he always looked so pleased.

We arrived at what seemed to be the front desk of the garage. It was covered with papers and work orders in progress. There was a calendar on the wall with all the past days marked off. A few people behind their desks were wearing dark blue uniforms with white name tags. My dad took me around and introduced me to one of them.

"Bob, come over here, I'd like you to meet my son."

The man began to approach. The man standing in front of me was enormous. He seemed like he stood seven feet tall and looked as if he weighed over 400 pounds. His muscles were bulging out of his shirt. They probably did not make uniforms in his size! Just when I was about to be tempted to run away, he reached out and shook my hand.

"It's nice to meet you, young man," he said in a surprisingly soothing voice.

"Bob here runs the shop. If we ever have car problems, he's the one to go to," Dad informed me.

Although he was so much larger than my dad, he really seemed to respect him. He gave my father his full attention as he was speaking. As they began to discuss some business, I took the opportunity to look at what was going on around the shop. I did not know how successful my dad was until I saw him working with these people. I had thought he was a good man who ran a good company. I realized later in life, it was his outward display of character that motivated these workers.

"Ok, Tom, do you want to see where all the magic happens?"

"Are you going to sell a car?"

"That's always a possibility."

I was excited. This is what I was waiting for all day; to be a part of a sale. I would be right next to my dad doing what he does best. As we walked, I decided that there was nothing in the world I would rather do than to eventually work with my dad and work for his company.

We went through the double doors that led to the showroom. Despite the slow business, I was still optimistic. Many sons probably would have found themselves to be quite bored with the situation. I continued to sit there for a few hours hoping for a tide of customers. My optimism was slowly fading.

"Tom, business is slow today; do you want to go out for lunch?"

"Sure, Dad, I'm sure business will pick up tomorrow," I stated as if I had been there on a regular basis!

As we drove away to lunch that day I looked back through the rear window at the building. It was a large work place with so many employees, but to me it was like a second home. It faded away in the distance but my day with my dad was not over yet.

We parked and headed into a local restaurant. The hostess greeted us and took us to a table in the back for two. It was a chance to talk to my dad one on one without any interruptions.

"So, Tom, how was your first day?"

"It was alright, but I was hoping to be a part of more important things."

"You will one day, I promise," my dad stated in a very serious way. "Tom, I know you want to be a part of everything, but you need to enjoy being in school and working hard to get here."

"I will, but this is what I want to do," I answered.

"I know you do, but we all have to wait for things we really want. To be in my situation it took many years of hard work and dedication. I have always wanted to do this but I was not able to be in this position until later in my life."

"Dad, I have a question," I interrupted.

"Yes, what is it?"

"Why are you so nice to everyone?"

He smiled. "Over the years of working and going to school I have learned a lot of things about people. In business and in life you need to be able to communicate well with others about what you want them to do. I have found that by being genuine and sincere people take you more seriously. By showing people you care, they care about what they do and then you find that you have a good business."

"What about that time you yelled at that man?" I asked him.

"I didn't yell at anyone; I may have raised my voice a little but that's just because he didn't show as much effort as I put into my part of the work. Although I may come off as being kind to everyone, there are still times when you need to show other emotions to get your point across."

At the time, I did not fully understand what my dad meant. However, that conversation would stay with me for years to come. My dad wore his heart on his sleeve knowing that it is out there for everyone to see. He had earned respect from people and he did it by showing them a tremendous amount of that same respect.

I would continue to visit my dad in his warm, lamp-lit office throughout the years of high school and college. He always found time for me as well as all the other people who came to his door. Everyone left that office with a smile that mirrored his smile. Dad was never truly away from home, as he extended the benefits of home to his workplace. I was proud to share in those benefits, and I am proud to be his son.

All of Us Have a Mission

Fathers can be there for us when we are about to leave the nest. They have been through that transition, and are able to share the wisdom of their experience. These military fathers see life as a mission. Missions are hard to plan alone and are more successful when they are worked out together. Sons worry about success. They want their fathers to be proud of them. These fathers have shown their sons to trust in themselves to find success. They do not judge them, but rather are delighted when their sons discover the mission for their lives!

The Father
He was on a mission...

Joining the Air Force had been a lifelong dream for me ever since I could remember. Whenever I would hear something on the radio or see a news program on television about this military element it would draw my attention. The pictures of my dad in his uniform covered the hallways of our house for my childhood years. My brother had made the commitment a few years ago and now I was about to follow him. I had always wanted to fly and I never seriously considered another career. It looked like the day was on the horizon.

Although it may seem like the military was imbedded into my thoughts ever since I was born, that is not the case. My dad did not serve for very long and my grandfather did not serve at all. The choice of the military profession was mine. I had always wanted to make the decision and I knew that it would make my dad proud.

We lived in the suburbs of a small community of about a thousand people. We woke up as a family every Sunday to get ready for church. My parents and I always went to church together. Today, it was a bit different; for it would be the last time I would be with them there for a long time. Tomorrow marked the first day of my military career. I could not believe that all the times we were sharing as a family were about to be something in my past.

While I was getting ready that morning I began taking into consideration what I was preparing to do. I was feeling a bit uneasy about moving away from home. We had a close knit family who often showed their love for each other. As my dad and I walked out to the car he put his hand on my shoulder and a sudden rush of fear filled me. I realized that sort of love and comfort would not be around much longer.

We pulled up as a family to the small Presbyterian church, a parish that could not have numbered more than a few hundred people, including membership from the neighboring towns. As we walked in, my dad headed over to discuss the details for the service that morning with our minister. My father was very involved in the church and served as an elder. He was a caring person in the community as well as in the home. He knew something about life and wanted to share it with everyone.

During the service I listened to my dad read the Scriptures. I paid close attention because I knew that I would not be hearing him read Scripture for a long time. As I looked at him I thought how effective was the life he lived. He had taught me lessons in so many ways. He had always led by example and had the right words to go with the situation. He probably learned this from his military experience. Dad served in World War II as a cadet officer in the Army Air Corps. When the war was over he came home and set aside the uniform for a civilian career. I wondered sometimes if he regretted that decision since the opportunities for travel were no longer possible. Throughout my childhood he had always taught me the ways of the military. We were asked to do chores every day and we would always be responsible for how well they were done. I had to complete more chores after my brother left the house, but I would never complain to the commanding officer!

When the service ended we remained for a while and talked with some people from the parish. Everyone knew I was leaving soon for the Air Force, so there were handshakes and hugs and well wishes. All of this attention did not help my feelings of uneasiness. With each hug the reality set in more and more that I was actually going away. Where would I end up? What sort of missions would I be given?

As we drove home in the car I needed to vent some of these feelings.

"Mom, Dad, I don't know what I'm getting myself into. Maybe the military isn't right for me," I said with a concern in my voice.

My parents had always been supportive in their parenting styles and they seemed to always handle these situations with seriousness. My mom probably did not really know what to say and may have felt that this was my dad's expertise. He had fought in a war, so he knew the experience first hand.

He responded with the perfect answer: "Ron, God has a plan for all of us, so you will do what He meant for you to do, whether it is in the military or not."

"Yes, but what if I am called to risk my life?" I asked.

"Actually, in the military there is only one thing, and that's completing the mission, whatever that mission should be. You're fighting for your country and doing what needs to get done. That is what it is all about."

"I know. I still want to go, I'm just sad to leave home," I said as we pulled into the driveway.

"Don't worry, it will be Ok," my mom chimed in, adding that motherly comfort when it was needed.

That day we had planned to go to the lake. It was something we did quite often during the summer weekends. We had a sixteen foot deck boat that we would tow into the lake a few miles down the road. Those times were some of the fondest memories I have of my father. We would be on the lake skiing, boating, fishing and anything else we would enjoy on a hot summer day. I was a little older, so our trips to the lake just consisted of lounging on the boat and maybe a quick dip. On a hot day like today that dip in the lake sounded very good.

We ran into the house to change into our summer wear and swim suits. I walked into my room and looked at my personal effects sitting there already packed. My parents planned to convert my room into a guest room. When I did come home, I would not be staying in "my room" anymore. My father believed that once you were eighteen and left for the Air Force, you were no longer a child in need of a room at home. I was about to become a man who was on his own.

As I changed into my swim trunks, I glanced at an old picture that my dad had given me. He was posed saluting in full uniform. He was a strong looking man and it seemed like there was pride in his eyes. He looked like he had been wearing that uniform for years. I looked at my empty room and started to think that maybe this would all be worth it. Maybe I could be the next service man in the picture and be as successful and happy as my father was now.

That afternoon's trip to the lake with my parents was a most relaxing time. We lowered the anchor in the middle of the lake and just let the boat turn in the wind. The lake was fairly large so the number of people that day did not take away from the quiet atmosphere. I sat in the driver's seat sprawled out tanning in the sun. As I lay there I was able to completely forget any concerns I had about the future.

Eventually I looked up and saw my dad who was lying on his stomach half asleep. I asked him the question that I had been wondering ever since I made my decision to go into the Air Force.

"Dad, what do you miss most about when you served?"

"There are a lot of things I miss, actually," my dad admitted with a sigh. "I miss the sense of mission. In the military everyone is working together for one common goal. That goal is to protect and fight for our country and to make the world a better place. We have our own tasks and group efforts and everyone is working hard."

"But you still have that at work, don't you?" I asked.

"Yes, but on a whole new level," he added as he laid there in the sun. "You see, today people just work for paychecks. Don't get me wrong. There are many people who work hard at their jobs. In my job many people I work for don't care about the job as much as we cared about our mission when we served. I formed a bond with many people and working with them was my life. I wanted to be there. When you serve, everyone is working towards something so much more important than money or individual gain. They are working for each other and for the betterment of everyone. It's the greatest mission of all and I miss that the most."

My father's memory of his military experience would be the basis for my career in the military. That was why for so many years he hinted at the idea of my joining the Air Force. He never forced the military life on me. He would have supported me in whatever I had decided to do. The military was the most logical because it was part of our family history and it could be a good formal education as well. With all of this said, my nerves were much calmer and I was now more excited to go than I had been before. That day my dad and I shared a memory that helped me to be more decisive about my career in the military. Although I was not sure about the situations I might face, the opportunity for success began to outweigh my doubts.

After a quick swim we decided to head back home for dinner. I kept in mind at each moment that this would be my last opportunity to be here as a civilian. When we took the boat out of the water and as when we drove home, I thought how much I would miss all those little things. At home I walked into my room again to see the empty shelves and the full suitcases.

My dad spent the next hour or two reading the paper in the living room while my mom cooked my last home cooked meal. I was upstairs busily loading things into the attic and getting ready for the next day. With that last seal of tape I was officially shutting out that part of my life and getting ready for a totally new one. I was no longer just playing with toy soldiers. I was about to become the real thing.

Dinner that night was a special event. That food seemed to taste better than it ever had before.

"Dad, you seem so happy tonight," I said, taken aback, knowing that I would not be there to see him regularly.

"I'm excited for you. It's not everyday a father gets to send his son off to the best military in the world. I'm proud of you." He was proud of me and he never had said that before. I had started the day a bit concerned, but now I was proud to serve my country like he had done.

That next day I started my career that would last twenty five years. I served in Vietnam, flying as a navigator in many missions. I lived the military life and moved all over the world having our first child in England and the second in Ohio. My military career was everything and more than my father told me it was going to be. Now that I have completed my career with the Air Force, I understand what my dad meant by "mission." We had so many missions throughout my career. Some were dangerous and some were even life threatening, but one thing was sure, everyone worked hard and worked together. The things my father told me he missed most, I now realize that I miss too. Today I work quality management at a plant and I see the type of workers to whom my father referred. In the military everyone was working hard for a common goal, whereas at a plant many only work for a paycheck. I received my work ethic from the military and I would not have it any other way. My father was a man who was able to complete his mission. Now that I have finished my military career, I know why my dad was so proud at the dinner table that night. He knew the satisfaction of completing the mission. Completing my mission has also made me a successful man.

Today, I see my children going through a similar experience. They both have chosen to go into the military as well. I could not be happier for them as their missions begin.

The Son
Facing the obstacles…

"Are you ready to go?" my dad asked as he was waiting in the kitchen, washing out his coffee mug.

"Yeah, yeah, I'm coming," I said as I looked in the mirror, making sure every inch of my appearance looked perfect for the big day. When you are headed to your state's capitol building for what may be one of the most important interviews of your life, you tend to be a little extra conscious about your appearance. Preparing for today had been causing me stress for quite some time. In order to be accepted into the Air Force Academy, I needed to be interviewed by a congressman. All of the other prospective cadets were to meet there as well.

"I'm just about ready. You can start the car," I yelled down the stairs to my dad so he wouldn't be annoyed.

Today was a big day for him as well. He had always thought that the Air Force was a great experience, and ever since I can remember I had wanted to attend there. He had never told me that I had to go, yet it seemed like I had made up my mind that this was the only choice. I believed that everyone should serve their country in some manner.

As I looked in the mirror I saw a face that was not prepared for the interview. I was dressed in a button down shirt that was firmly pressed the night before. My pants had the perfect pleat and there was nothing out of place on my entire body. Even though I may have looked the part, I still did not have the confidence that was necessary. When I finally walked down the stairs and said goodbye to my mother, I felt uncertain about my chances.

"Wish me luck Mom, I'm sure going to need it," I said with a sigh as I hugged her.

"Don't worry. You were made for this. Your father did it and your sister did it too. You'll be great honey."

My sister had just graduated from the Air Force Academy that past month. My parents were so proud of her. She finished near the top in her class. She had made a wooden case so that she could place her graduation saber with my dad's. They were hanging in the family room next to each other waiting for mine. I wanted nothing more than to hold that saber up high and to one day place it there.

None of this could happen if my interview did not go well today.

After some pointers from my mother about my posture and another hug, I headed out the garage door and into the waiting car. I was looking forward to this drive to the Capitol with my dad. It was familiar for him since he had done it himself and he drove my sister there as well. Ever since I was little he was the man with the answers. My earliest memory of my father was when we lived in Ohio and attended the air shows on the base. He could point to any plane in the sky and he would know the exact model and name. He would often even relate many other minor details about planes. Hopefully some of that wisdom and knowledge was passed down to me for this very important day.

We pulled out of the driveway and were silent for the first part of the journey. This was usual for communication with my father. We had not often been completely open with our feelings or emotions. When we did talk it was mostly about my sports teams or my involvement in other activities. We also spoke about the military and about the Academy. He loved the Academy. He had a very long career there, lasting twenty or thirty years. Before my sister had attended, he had not been to Colorado Springs in almost twenty years. Every year we would visit her on parent's weekend and my dad would enthusiastically look over the place once again. I remember seeing his face the last time we were there. He would walk off by himself just to see what was happening there. His military style walk and deportment made him look like he belonged there.

"So," my dad broke the silence after a few minutes, "do you have that folder with the list of things you are going to say?"

"Yes I do, right here," I said, holding the folder in the air. "What do you think I should say?" I asked, hoping that he would give me some of that wisdom he had stored.

. "How old are you now?" he responded with a bit of sarcasm in his voice.

"Eighteen," I said a little confused.

"Well, if you think you are going to make it into the Academy then you need to start making some decisions on your own," he said in a stern voice.

This answer surprised me because usually he would help me out with this sort of situation.

"When you leave school after you are eighteen you need to start making some decisions on your own. The bills are going to start coming and all those little things we've taught you over the years will prove useful. We can't be there to help you anymore. Now is the time to prove to yourself that you can do it."

With that said I felt a little confidence. Although it was not exactly what I wanted to hear, it had a good effect. My dad had always insisted that I do things on my own and had always wanted me to "grow up." Ever since I was required to do chores I had tried to finish a job without complaining. Today was no different. He was not going to give me the answer so I was going to have to find it on my own.

The rest of the car ride was spent in silence listening to the radio. We arrived in about forty minutes. I was ready. I had practiced the night before and had everything scripted. We walked through the big double doors at the capitol building toward the waiting room. Usually there are about five or six people who attend and three or four of them are accepted. As I turned the corner into the room I stared in horror at the group. There were nine candidates and I knew three of them. Two of them were honor students and were already accepted into the academy. I knew the third had an incredible transcript. I looked around and saw six other candidates and I felt that my work was cut out for me.

I waited there with my dad. Why had these people chosen to go this year? I needed to give the interview of my life. When they called my name, I barely heard it for all the thoughts that were racing through my head. As I walked out of the room I looked over at my father who simply gave me a nod and a small smile.

I felt that I had given a good interview. I answered all the questions and those answers seemed to be accepted by the congressman. I walked out of the room with confidence knowing that I did my best and that I had done it on my own

I said to my father: "I think I did alright."

We drove home talking about the numerous parts of the interview. I was telling him about a few questions that gave me some difficulty and asked him how he would have answered them. He answered the questions in a similar fashion, but I still wondered if I had given enough to be accepted, in light of the competition. After a while, we returned to the usual silence as we listened to the radio.

The next week or two continued with little or no discussion about the interview. I was prepared for the worst because I knew what I was up against. After I saw the competition, I began researching colleges who had good ROTC programs. I had already applied and was accepted for two of them. I just needed to prioritize and be sure I knew which school was the best. Even though I knew that my chances for the Academy were not very good, I still thought in the back of my mind that I could be accepted. My dad and my sister had attended there, so how could I go anywhere else?

I had been picking up the mail for the past few days knowing that notification would come soon. As soon as I saw the envelope I would know the decision. An envelope was bad news, a packet was good news. I went out to the mail box that Saturday morning. As I looked through the mail I stared in horror at one envelope. It was the envelope. I did not even have to open it. It had my name written in blue and the Air Force Academy's logo stamped on the upper left corner.

I went inside and told the news to my parents. I could not help the tears. I thought I was prepared for it, but the reality was different. My dad patted my shoulder as I sat there in the kitchen. He knew how I felt as he probably felt the great disappointment too. So many questions went through my head. What do I do now? Was the interview a failure? Why did the competition have to be so hard this year? The case with the sabers will only contain two. It would be my father that would help me through this tough time. He encouraged me to proceed to the next step.

We went upstairs to begin to make a decision about which ROTC program I should attend.

"Dad," I said catching my breath as we searched the internet, "I'm sorry to let you down."

"Don't say that," my dad said in a concerned voice. "You did your best and that's all that matters. You are still going to serve your country and be a pilot. Don't give up just because one school tells you that you can't go there."

"I know, but I've heard what Debbie says about all the ROTC grads. She laughs at them. And I'm going to be one of them," I said, realizing it as I said it.

"Don't worry. When I left the academy I met many people who went through great ROTC programs. Some of the finest working people I ever met went through the ROTC program. Some think that it is better because you are able to live more of a college life and then you can concentrate fully on the military life that comes after it."

"But that's not the way you wanted me to go, is it?" I asked somewhat confused.

"Listen. I don't care where you go as long as you do your best. I do think that the military and the Air Force are a good start for a person of your age and will give you a good basis for life. The academy is only one path that closed of many that you may choose."

I looked at my dad's face and he genuinely cared. For some reason I never thought he wanted me to go anywhere else. He continued to talk like he was excited for me to accept one of the ROTC programs. He never seemed to care about my schooling as much as he did now. It was almost as if he wanted to be in my shoes and make the decision again.

We continued to research and look at schools on the internet. We looked at the different campuses and noted what the programs offered. We joked about the school mascots and we talked about how it would be easy to find other schools. It is ironic to realize that one of the worst mornings in my life turned around to be one of the best memories I have of my father. It was also one of the best afternoons I had ever spent with him.

"What would you do in my situation?" I said having no clue what he would say back.

"In your situation, I probably would do the exact same thing. I would look at other programs and find a different path. I would make the next path the best path. In life," he continued, "you'll find that there are always obstacles, and you have had a big one. What will make or break you is how you handle the obstacles. In the military you will face many barriers and there you learn the skills necessary to overcome them."

He wanted me to learn on my own. He was allowing me to be an adult. It was a very special moment between my father and I as we bridged the gap between my childhood and adulthood.

He taught me that life does not always just pitch you a ball to smack out of the park. It throws curve balls, high balls and fast balls; and sometimes you may strike out. But there is another inning. The key to life is taking those tough pitches and still finding a way to win. It did not matter where I went to school or which military life I chose, as long as I found out what best suited my life and my strengths. He had taught me what it meant to succeed and how I needed to work to be successful.

Since that day, each time I have faced an obstacle, my father's wisdom has been with me. No matter what path I have to take, I am headed toward success!

Building a New Life

No one escapes the experience of the death of someone they love. Fathers and sons have their time to grieve and, if they are fortunate, their time to make amends. A new life can be built and passed on to a new generation. The men in these stories experience death not as an end of a relationship, but the ground upon which much can be built. Fathers can teach their sons how to build on a more solid foundation, just as they have learned to be builders of a new life for themselves.

The Father
When a life ends...

As I gazed out the window I could not help but to notice how beautiful a day it was. It was a late summer afternoon with a few clouds in the sky and a slight breeze; a perfect day to be outside. I was not out there and I could not be.

For the past few weeks I had been having the time of my life. I had a good group of friends. We went to parties together and I was playing sports as well. It was all about to catch up with me in an instant.

"Martin, stop looking out that window and look at me!" the teacher behind the desk snapped.

She was our school principal; not a very gentle woman, but fair to most of us. She had just received notice from my teachers that I was failing most subjects. It was no shock for me, and I did not care. At that point in my life, school just was not high on my list of priorities. We lived on a farm, so my "home work" was there. When I arrived at school I did not want to work anymore. Apparently, teachers and administrators did not agree with my logic, especially at this private school.

"Why haven't your parents given me that note back?" she asked me as I began looking out the window again.

"They don't care; they got it and threw it out." I lied to her.

"Well maybe they'll care when you aren't allowed to come back," she added in a matter-of-fact tone.

"Are you serious?" I asked as I stood up to confront her.

"Yes I am, and I hope you find something in life in which you can succeed because this school has had enough."

I walked out of the room. I could not believe my luck at being kicked out of school. This is perfect. Now I could get out of this private school and join up with all of my friends in the public school. Not only will I be able to see them all, but now I could play football and wrestle, something I could not do at this private school.

It was a forty five minute walk to return home and I was glad to have the time to prepare an explanation for my parents. I would have to make a good sales pitch for my plan to work. They really had no idea how I was doing in school and probably did not even see this coming. I continued on the dirt road to our small country house.

As I walked up to the front door I could not help but think what my dad would say. I began to feel a bit guilty about what I had done. They would probably ground me for life! Dad has always been a strict father, punishing me for my wrongdoings. It was my hope that he would decide to send me to the public school.

I went into the living room where both my parents were sitting on the couch. I found out soon enough that they knew what had happened and they were there waiting for me. This was not good. All of the reasons and the points I had listed in my headed suddenly vanished.

"Sorry, I should have told you," I squeezed out, knowing I had just been caught red handed.

"Go to your room," my dad stated in a surprisingly calm voice.

I had six siblings and there was never a place in that house where you could be alone. As I walked into our room my brother was sitting there on his bed. He knew something had happened because my dad usually was not inside during the day. He would have normally been out working in the fields.

"You must have really done something this time," my brother said in a voice that hinted he was glad it was me and not him.

"Hopefully this works and I can get out of that school. Mom and Dad should just send me to the public school," I explained.

"They might not. Your plan could backfire like it usually does."

My brother was probably right. But I hated being at that school and I wanted to be around more students and play more sports. I knew I would have more chance for that at a new school. However, my dad was such a religious man that I do not think he would just pull me out of a Catholic school without a good reason.

As I lay there in my bed, I began to have second thoughts about what I had done in the past few weeks.

Dad had been in and out of the hospital for the past year. He had extremely high blood pressure and had undergone surgery for that condition. To make matters worse, a few months ago he was in a car accident where he received the brunt of the injuries. Only recently had he been able to continue working on the farm. I waited with my thoughts for about an hour when finally my dad entered my room. He had obviously been talking to Mom for quite some time.

"Excuse us, Jason, I need to talk to your brother," my dad explained.

The next few words were the only words that were ever said about the issue. The conversation didn't last long but it is one of the clearest memories I have of my father.

"Listen, you need to get this straightened out with school. Seeing you like this is really hurting your mother."

He said nothing about himself. All he said was is that it hurt my mother. I did not understand it. I thought I was going to get the scolding of a lifetime and an earful concerning how I let him down. But all he said was that it hurt my mother. It seemed like he knew exactly where to hit a nerve. At this point I had completely erased any thought of going to another school.

"Don't worry, I'll get you one more chance and I'll talk to the school."

And he did. He went in the next afternoon and before I knew it I was back at school. The slate had been erased. He had always been a generous, caring guy but you could not really see it on the outside. He was a man of action. Within a few months I was able to pull my grades back together.

Later that same fall, my father was back in the hospital with more blood pressure problems. This time they were more serious. He had to stay there for a few weeks. Doctors told us they were unable to make the blood pressure go down. We soon began to realize that my father was dying.

Our family spent so much time in that hospital the last few weeks of his life. Every time we entered his room he looked happier to see us. Each of us would get about an hour per day to visit one on one with him and we would talk about what was going on in our lives at school and at home.

After a while I knew most of the people on his floor. As

I walked through the halls I would greet the receptionists and the nurses. I turned the corner into my dad's room to see him lying there. Even though he was weak, he still smiled a broad smile. I put my hand on his arm as I usually did. I did not feel very comfortable hugging him just because I had not really hugged him since I was a child. I could tell from the look on his face that he had something to tell me today.

"Dad, you're looking great," I said.

"Yes, well I guess you can probably take me wrestling now," he forced out.

"So have you seen anybody else today?" I asked.

"Yes, but I really needed to talk to you." My dad's smile turned into a serious expression almost instantly.

"Yeah, Dad, I'm here," I said in a confused voice. One might think that the next words out of his mouth would be about some life lesson or some moment of truth. In a way it was.

"Son, I need you to do one thing for me."

"Yes, Dad," I replied, "I'll do anything.

"I need you to take care of your mother," he said.

"With me gone, you and your brothers are going to have to keep up the farm and look after your mom."

It was about my mom again. At the time I felt like he did not really care about anything as much as my mother. On his deathbed, he just wanted to be sure my mom was going to be alright. I then looked at my dad and replied, "Don't worry about anything, Mom will be fine, and we'll all be taking care of her."

The rest of the afternoon we spent together chatting about other things of interest to him. We talked about what he was like when he was my age and what he thought I should do for college. We talked about my brothers and my sister and what he thought they would eventually choose for their vocations. Before I knew it, I had been there for a few hours. It was the first afternoon in my life where I spent that much time talking with my father.

My sister had arrived to spend a little time with him too. He turned to me once more on my way out.

"Remember, please make sure you take care of your mother." He looked me straight in the eyes as if these were his last words.

It turned out they were indeed his last words to me. The next day he lapsed into a coma and a few days later my father passed away. I was only fourteen years old and it felt like I barely had the opportunity to know him. I am glad that there were those last few weeks with him and a time where we could begin to understand each other better.

We continued to work on the farm and take care of my mother as I had promised. She struggled at being alone but was strong when she needed to be. I would like to think that strength came with my help. It would have been the way Dad wanted it.

I have been now blessed with a wonderful wife, two sons and a daughter. A shattering experience had clearly brought back memories of my father. My wife became very ill with lung cancer. She never smoked a day in her life, yet she was plagued with the disease when my youngest son was sixteen and my older twins were headed off to college. It was a devastating blow to our entire family. She was the backbone of us all, and when she knew that the end was near, she became very sentimental towards me and towards everyone. She told us to take care of each other. She would talk about those special moments that we shared together. One of the last memories I have of her was as she lay in the hospital bed she wanted the assurance that I would take care of our children. I have always kept that promise to my wife. From that moment I would be involved in their lives more than ever. I keep in touch with them even though two of them live in other cities.

As I experienced this death, I remembered my father. I watched as my children experienced it as well and I understood their reactions. I realized how important she was in my life and how I would have done anything to keep her here for them and for me. My father had the same sort of love for my mother. I see the caring and the love one can have for the other. I once thought that it was because my dad loved my mom more than us. I now realize that I was wrong. It was simply a different kind of love.

When people get married they make a bond that will last forever. That bond will always hold strong, even through death. Although my dad was going to pass away, he wanted Mom to be safe, because he knew she would always have that bond.

Now I look back on my dad and his life in a completely different light. I look at the good times and I focus on the pleasant memories. I know that I still have an opportunity to share memories with my children. It has been a wonderful experience watching them grow and pursue their own careers. I know my father would have been proud of them.

I now realize that some of the most valuable lessons I have learned have come from my father. With time, I have come to value my experiences with him. My father will always hold a special place in my heart and it is my hope that my children might be able to say the same.

The Son
Dad and I build together...

"When is dad coming home?" I asked my mom yelling from the garage.

"He should be home in an hour, why don't you come in and eat something before he gets here?" my mom suggested.

"No, I have to get ready," I said as I rearranged the tools.

Mom was not in the best of health lately. She was keeping up the front of being strong, but I had seen her health ebb away, especially in the last few months. None of us wanted to face the possibility of her death. When I was with my father, I hoped that his projects would distract me from that reality.

I had been looking forward to this for the entire week. My dad said that we were going to do a family project together. We would build a deck on the house in our backyard. A project like this was not very common as we never seemed to have time for such things. When Dad arrived home, I wanted to be ready.

My dad and I have had an interesting relationship over the years. We had never really talked much, but I usually enjoyed his company. He was a strict man and many of the memories I have of my childhood are times of discipline. I probably deserved it. He was strict because he needed to be and did a good job in enforcing the rules at home. This would be my opportunity to show my dad what I could do as we worked on a project together.

I was only sixteen years old and I really did not know where to start. As I made one last check to see if all the nails were there and the wood was lined up neatly outside, I heard the garage door opening. It was he.

He was a slim man who enjoyed outdoor activities. We played tennis regularly, and we had a family membership at the tennis courts and golf course nearby. I have many memories of playing tennis and golf with my father, but I never had been so excited to really show him what I could do.

"Hi, Dad," I said as I walked up to the car, "I have every-thing ready to go."

"Good. Let me get changed and we can get started," he said.

My father worked so hard every day and I always thought that he had a tiring job. Whenever he would talk about his life he would say how easy it is now compared to years ago. I remember him telling me stories about how he only had two shirts. One was for church and the other for school. He told me how hard he worked on the farm. Maybe that was why he was always assigning chores to us!

The tools were ready to go and I was ready to build this deck with my dad. My older brother would probably help too, but I knew that he had plans to go out with his friends that night. I did not want him to help as this was supposed to be my special project.

Dad walked into the garage. He was wearing those same blue jeans that he wore every time he worked in the yard. They were a sight for sore eyes; mostly because they reminded me of warm summer days. He seemed to be in a better mood when he wore those jeans. Maybe we all were as well!

We started our project by measuring out the area on which we would build and set up markers. It was my first job and I wanted it to be perfect. As I measured I would make sure that it was. He would look over occasionally and give me a smile. This little gesture went a long way. My father was not much of a talker, so when he reacted like this it always meant a great deal to me. I knew I was doing a good job.

"Do you have that all measured over there?" he asked me as I staked out my last area.

"Yep, all done," I said as I pounded in the last stake.

"Good," my dad said, "grab that pencil out of my tool box and help me measure some of this."

My dad was an accountant and was very good with numbers. Ever since I can remember, he helped me with math or balanced our family checkbook. He always wanted everything to balance perfectly and I expected the measurements would also be nothing short of perfect.

He turned to me and asked, "Would you grab the other pencil and help me mark some of this wood?"

"Really," I asked in complete confusion, "I might mess something up."

"As long as you are careful, you should be fine," he assured me.

This was definitely a surprise. Usually, my dad never let me do anything but the tedious easy work. He had made me feel important and I felt more a part of the project. I watched him measure and tried to mimic his way of measuring. We decided to have everything lined up so we could saw all of the pieces at the same time. He was including me so much that I felt a true sense of accomplishment. Although we did not say much as we worked, that sense of accomplishment went beyond just the deck. I felt good about being treated more like an adult.

Before I knew it, it was nine o'clock. We had finished all of the measurements and he said that this was a good place to stop.

"So you ready to call it a night?" he asked.

"Yes, I'm getting real tired." I confessed.

We went inside and showered and prepared for bed.

That day had been one of the best days I had spent with my dad. We both went to sleep quickly as we knew that there would be a long day ahead of us.

He woke me up bright and early to get started for the day. He had been an early riser, so he probably had already been up a while before he woke me.

"It's time to get up," he said in a soft voice, "we need to get started."

We ate our breakfast together that morning, at an hour long before most people wake up.

"Ok, we're going to start by sawing these pieces," my dad explained. "Will you go get the saw in the garage?" I found myself enthusiastic about the project and I was so happy that he was including me. First, we needed to hand-saw the posts that would go into the ground. I watched as he completed the first one. He did it to perfection and not once did he go off the line that was penciled onto the wood. Just as the block of wood hit the floor I looked up at him and he was holding the saw out for me to take from him.

"Oh, no Dad," I said in total disbelief, "you can do that, I'll do something else."

"No, it's Ok, you can do it."

I really did not want to. I could destroy his perfect measurements. Yesterday I had done the job well and I did not want to change that track record. As I placed the saw on the slab of wood I took a deep breath and told myself that I would be fine. I thought that this is where I was going to prove that I could do this.

Looking down, I could see that I was doing a good job. It was not nearly as clean a line as his, and it took me twice as long to saw it, but after a minute or two of cutting, I had indeed done a good job.

"Well done, that's not too bad for your first time," he encouraged me.

And I was glad. My dad was encouraging me to get the job done right. This was turning out to be a great day! We continued sawing the different pieces we would need to finish framing the deck.

We were cutting for much of the morning. I can not remember any specific conversation, but I remember feeling focused and satisfied with the work I was doing.

Once the pieces were cut, my dad turned to me and asked, "What do you say we do next?"

I did not know what to say. He was the one who was the expert.

"I guess we could start nailing them together," I said in a timid voice.

"Right, let's do that," my dad said with much enthusiasm.

I could not believe that he had just included me in such an important decision! It made me feel that he trusted me and believed that I now could do the work.

We sat there for most of the afternoon hammering away. I looked over at my dad in his favorite jeans to see him smiling. He was working hard, but I could see a little smile and knew that he was satisfied with the project. We were making a memory together that was more important to me than this deck. We were accomplishing something together and that feeling of accomplishment would last.

At the dinner table later that night I let the entire day sink in. We finished the deck the next day. I was now more confident using the little lessons in construction I had learned from him.

Mom went into the hospital a week later. What had been announced as a period of tests became a time to realize that she was not coming home. She was able talk one last time to all of us, even though we did not want to say goodbye to her. On my last visit she smiled as I entered the room.

"Here comes the deck builder," she said. "You and your father are quite the team."

We had become a team. I believe that she knew our team was able to continue without her, even though we would miss her deeply.

The memory of my father and I building our deck together, a deck that still sits there today ten years later, is a memory I will continue to cherish. We still talk today about those father and son events. He remembers building that deck with me as the time we bonded as father and son. I feel that I can accomplish so much because of my father's encouragement and commitment to me. Our activities over the years gave me a sense of accomplishment and self confidence to begin new projects on my own. Today, I work with my father at his accounting practice. I know that working along side of him I will continue to be encouraged in my goals of life.

The Stature of Liberty

Sons watch as their fathers relate to others and they watch as others react to their fathers. Only a man of great stature has so many friends and makes such a great difference in the life of his son. A young man is rightly full of pride and he matures well in such an environment. Fathers can be the best salesmen. They have the ability to make their sons feel loved, respected and accepted. Together they can grow in stature to experience the liberty of happy and healthy individuals.

The Father

His friends called him Bedloe...

My parents had five children. We all learned to love Boston and everything about it. We were Celtic fans and Red Sox fans and we loved our home teams. Rituals were dear to my father. It was New Year's Day, and our house had just been the site of a very big party.

"What a night this had been," I heard my mom saying to my dad in the kitchen.

"Yes," he said, "things did get a little crazy."

Our home had always been a gathering place for my parents and their friends. The biggest occasion was January 1. Being Irish Catholic and growing up on the north side of Boston, could have meant that our St. Patrick Day party would have been even bigger. However, every New Year's morning we would get together as a family and cook omelets for all those friends, relatives and neighbors who would come to our home. It was not uncommon to have close to one hundred people that morning for the brunch. It was a good thing it was only 6:30 in the morning. I had a paper route where I delivered about a hundred papers around the neighborhood. Usually I would do it alone with my bike, but on the weekends my dad would take me. I always looked forward to this weekly ritual.

"Dad," I began to ask as he got in the car, "why do we always have to have everything at our house?"

"Well," my dad started to explain, "we do get invited to other places and today it is my turn to say thank you to all of those people who were gracious to us over the year."

That made sense. My dad was often visiting his friends on the weekends. He was the life of the party. They had a nickname for him. "Bedloe." I never completely understood from where that came or what it meant, but all of his friends called him by that name.

It was a cold morning and we had just received another few inches of snow the night before. I had to deliver the Boston Globe to everyone in our neighborhood. I was not complaining. It was good money for a twelve year old. I think my dad enjoyed being able to spend a morning with me every week. He even helped me on this busy morning.

"So do you think we can break our old record of 45 minutes?" he asked as we pulled out of the driveway.

"I think we can do it," I said as I prepared to open the car door for the first delivery of the day.

It was a leisurely morning for him. He sat and read the paper as he drove slowly down the street with me doing all of the running. Occasionally he would throw some of the papers to me and we would work together.

He was so caring and helpful that he made my childhood a great experience. It was probably because he was such a kid at heart. Whatever the reason, it made my life much better. My siblings would always give me a hard time because they thought I was my dad's favorite. Now that I think about it, I probably was. We shared many of the same interests and we both had the same sense of humor. I did not mind their teasing, as long as I could spend more time with 'Bedloe.'

Before long we had finished the entire neighborhood. It always took less time when my dad drove, especially in the winter. Now that this job was over, the bigger one was about to begin.

My dad asked us to dress up and serve as the waiters and waitresses for the party. For the few days prior to the brunch, Dad would spend hours in the kitchen chopping up every possible ingredient you could imagine. He even had brought in an additional stove with a big griddle and a silver canopy-like cover.

"So, what job are you going to do this year?" he asked me as we pulled into the house.

"I don't know, hopefully take their orders. It's always interesting to see the different ingredients people like," I told him.

It was only about nine o'clock and we still had some time before the first arrivals. I still had to shower and get dressed. My sister was usually the one who took coats as she was the youngest. My older brothers would take orders with me and Mom would refill drinks and make sure everyone was comfortable.

The orders would go on for an hour. I remember people calling out their appreciation to my father. After the first wave of orders, I had a few minutes to relax on the couch. I sat next to one of my dad's best friends.

"You all put on a real nice brunch every year," the man complimented me.

"Yeah, Dad really loves having everyone," I responded.

"You are very lucky to have a dad like that," the man continued. "Someone who cares that much about other people must care about his own family a lot too."

Before then, I had never really thought about it. He did love his friends, but he did spend time doing things with his family as well. He would include us at his parties and we had a home where we knew we were loved. He was a traveling salesman who was very good at his job and, on occasion, he even took me on his business trips around the area.

Just then, a loud group of people we knew walked in. I went back and informed my dad that they were there.

"Dad, the Douglas family is here and they're as loud as ever," I informed him as I slid their order slip into the metal slab above the griddle.

"Don't worry about them. Just be sure they are welcome. You'll meet a lot of people with whom you may not get along. You just have to act like it doesn't bother you and forget about it. Look at all of the great people here. When you show them hospitality and caring, they might just be affected for the good by it."

I did not expect to get such a lecture from my dad while he was busy cooking. But I did think about the many different types of people there. He had many friends, so I am sure that advice was sound. Dad did not always have the time to give me these lessons on growing up. On occasion, he had scolded me for doing what was wrong and he had often complimented me for the things that I did right.

After a few hours he turned off the griddle and began mingling with the guests. I was out on the deck when a person asked him a question that captured my attention.

"So Bedloe, if you had a million bucks, how would you live?"

"Well," my dad said looking around the grounds and at the house, "probably something like this."

I did not understand that answer. We were not the richest of folks, but we could definitely upgrade our house and do a lot with a million dollars. Yet he was happy with the life he had made. He had no regrets and I respected him for that. He was as peaceful as a man could be with fifty people walking throughout your house! My father had truly made our home a place of special welcome to others.

"What about you, young man, what do you want to be when you grow up?" a man, who obviously had a few too many drinks asked, turning the attention my way.

"Well, I've never really thought about it," I said.

"You should think about going into sales. You and your dad both have that charming personality. You'd be good at it."

It did not mean much coming from this man who was practically falling over on the sofa, but it make me begin to think about it. I was only twelve at the time and I did admire my father and his work ethic. It did sound like a job that I would enjoy. I could be traveling the country, meeting people and seeing many places.

From that point on, I never really gave serious consideration to choosing another type of work. My father had told me about his work and his travels over the years, but I do not think he did so to encourage me to follow in his footsteps.

It was now about two o'clock and people were beginning to leave. Dad stood by the door to greet everyone as they left the house. You could tell by the way he shook their hands and wished them well that he was truly glad they were able to attend. He was the reason people kept coming back every year.

Today I have taken on the role of father. My son is entering college and I look forward to watching him grow and develop into an adult. My father died too early and was not able to see that transition. I look forward to developing a more adult relationship with my son, one where he can look to me as a friend as well as a father.

In every sales pitch that I use, in every party that I host, I try to be like my father. I finally discovered the meaning of his nickname. He had reminded his friends of our national monument on "Bedloe's" Island. He continues to be a light and encouragement for me to make my son and the people in my life always feel welcome.

The Son
The Island was the highlight...

One might think that being an only child means spending unlimited time with your parents. Well that was not the case for me. My father was a traveling salesman, so I saw him less than most sons were able to see their dads. My parents told me many years ago that I had been adopted, but I never felt that made any difference in our lives. As the years passed I realized that I did want to develop a special bond with my dad. While I was in the eighth grade the opportunity arose to spend one special weekend with him.

The trip had been planned for a few weeks and I was excited in anticipation. Even though I had not been very vocal about my excitement, I am sure that he knew that I was looking forward to the weekend. He still traveled often, but his office was at home. By that point in my life I occupied myself with many middle school social activities. But this weekend would be just for us. Our plan was to go to one of the most exciting cities in the world. He had taken me with him on a few small and nearby trips before, and we had a good time on those trips, but I have never hoped to be able to go all the way to New York. Ever since I could remember, my dad had made an honest effort to attend all of my sports functions and school activities. To be able to go with him to a place of his choosing would be a special time for me to appreciate his interests.

"So Dad, what are we going to do first?" I asked as we were loading the luggage into the car.

"Well, I have some work to do later this afternoon in New Jersey and then tomorrow we'll be in New York for the fun part," he told me.

"When are we going to go to Times Square?" I asked hoping for the possibility of getting on television.

"We'll see when we get there," he said, "There are so many fun places. New York has everything!"

I knew it did. That's why I was so excited. To see the Statue of Liberty, Chinatown, the business district; it all sounded so exciting. Dad grew up on the east coast, so he had been to New York often.

"Wow," my dad said, looking out the window of the plane, "look at how small all the boats are."

He never missed an opportunity to be humorous. He was always telling stories and has probably told more jokes in his lifetime than most people. He was such a social person and everyone seemed to like him. He was friendly when he met strangers and he made them smile. It was no different around the house. He was always teasing my mom and making her laugh.

When we got off the plane we went directly to our hotel. It was one of those huge, old-fashioned buildings that I had seen in the movies many times. As we entered the lobby, I noticed my dad saying hello to everyone he met. He had obviously been there before.

"Hello, Mr. Snyder." The receptionist greeted him.

"Hello, how are you today?" he asked her sincerely, as he usually does with anyone he greets.

"I'm fine, but it seems your room isn't available," she said in a surprisingly upbeat tone. "But we do have one room available. I'm sorry to inform you that it's the Presidential Suite!"

I could not believe it. They gave my dad, the traveling salesman, the Presidential Suite. They treated him like royalty, like he was the most important man in the world. I did not understand it. We had become like royalty for the night and I was going to enjoy every minute of it.

When we arrived at the room I turned to my dad and asked him, "How come everyone knows you so well? And why did they give us the Presidential Suite?"

"Well, as long as your good to people they will always make things easier for you. If they ever visited us, I would act the same. The weekend is ours, now what should we do first?" My dad was putting everything aside and let me choose all of our activities together. That was a wonderful feeling.

"We need to catch a cab into town." We took the elevator to the lobby, left our hotel and within seconds a cab pulled up and was ready to go. He gave the driver explicit directions and after a fairly long ride we arrived at our destination. As I stepped out of the cab I realized we had driven down to the end of Manhattan. There, in front of me was New York harbor.

"Oh, look! I want to see the Statue of Liberty," I explained, "It's something I've always wanted to do!"

"Sounds good to me," my dad said in immediate agreement.

We purchased tickets for the ferry and enjoyed the short ride to the island. The statue seemed to grow in size as we approached. It was one of the most amazing sights I have ever seen. We took the elevator up to the deck and looked back to the city. I was finally at one of our country's most historic landmarks. We talked about the history of the statue. He told me about the time that he first visited there. He seemed proud to be able to share in my first experience.

"This is our beacon of freedom," he beamed. "All of us

have a right to that freedom. It is part of us, it is our heritage."

I could see that the celebration of freedom was an important part of his life. I imagine he recalled the voice of his own father. Grandpa was a great salesman as well, and Dad wanted to be like him. We looked up at the statue once again. I thought of the many immigrants she greeted on their way to a new land. Our stories were not much different. I began to realize that my father's gift for me was the same gift he had received from his father. He had made me feel welcome, a part of his family, even though,as an adopted son, I could have been treated like an outsider. That approach would have been foreign to him. He gave me the gift of growing in stature alongside him. Bedloe's Island will always remind me of that and forever be the highlight of our journey together.

It was about two in the afternoon when we returned to the city. We decided that this would be a good time to see the business district. We wanted to be there before five o'clock to avoid the rush hour. We looked for another cab and my dad used his extremely loud whistle.

"Where did you learn how to whistle like that?" I asked him.

"Actually my dad taught me. Do you want to learn?"
He sat there in the cab and tried to teach me. My dad had always been amusing company, but during this trip I was really beginning to see my dad as a friend. Many sons grow up never having such an opportunity.

On our arrival we looked into the windows of the Stock Exchange. It was interesting to see all of the people doing their jobs. Dad talked to me about his job and also about the work his father had done. He went into many details about his experiences at my age. It felt good knowing more about his experiences with my grandfather.

Later, we hailed another cab to Chinatown. Dad enjoyed talking with the vendors on the streets and bargaining with them. Many people would ignore vendors as they walked past, but not my dad. He would make eye contact even if it was just to say, "No thank you". It made sense that he treated people like this because he had always taught me that everyone is equal and deserves to be treated with respect. After the brief visit there we decided to return to our hotel. There had been much about my father's life that I never knew and I was happy to hear his stories and that he wanted his son to know about them. We went back to the hotel to get ready for a night on the town.

"If you want to change you had better hurry," he said.

"We want to get to Times Square in time to see the lights, have some dinner and one more surprise!"

It did not take me long to be ready and we were soon outside and walking up Broadway towards Times Square. I was amazed at the amount of lights and the crowds of people. The lights reflected off my father's face as he enjoyed this walk and seemed to delight in my reactions. He chose a restaurant on one of the side streets where he said the food was excellent and the service was better. That night at dinner we talked about my plans for the future. I was comfortable talking with my dad about such things. "You have some time before all those decisions will have to be made," he told me.

He smiled and slipped into my hand tickets for a Broadway show. I gasped as I realized they were front and center.

"Well, let's be off, we don't want them to give away our seats!"

It was a wonderful night that brought a wonderful day to a close. I look back upon this trip as the time when my relationship with my dad came of age. The two days of that weekend marked the beginning of my adult years. Dad assisted me in that process. Today, I value the unique relationship that we share. My father is a man of great stature. I thank him for giving me the freedom to grow in stature alongside him.

My Dad, My Hero

Heroes take many forms. Sons look up to their fathers for guidance and for strength. Sometimes the roles may be reversed. The first son in this story cared for his father and through that caring realized not only the hero in his dad, but the hero he too could become. In turn, he supported his son and coached him through life. His son had reason to truly admire his father as a role model. These men become heroes together and heroes for each other.

The Father
Relying on my strength...

It had been such a long hard winter on all of us. Between my demanding job and my son's sports schedule, we barely had enough time to make the drive to Detroit to see my father. Dad was sick with stomach and liver cancer and was only given a year to live.

At the time I was working as a journalist for many different magazines and I also had responsibilities for my church. My oldest son, nine years old at the time, was involved in tennis that consumed most of his weekends. This particular weekend was one of the more hectic ones. I decided to miss both one son's track meet and the other son's tennis lessons. My father had become increasingly ill over the past few weeks and I felt a sense of urgency to go to him.

Most of the time, our drive back home with the family in tow was a long one. This time I was alone with the silent rain lightly pelting the car. It was peaceful and I took that opportunity to reflect on my father's life. Over the past few years of his illness, I had begun reflecting quite often. This time was no different.

I always began by thinking of the memories that might have seemed to others to be of little significance. I do not have many memories of my father from earlier in life simply because he was not there very often. I barely knew him in my early childhood. At the time, I did not understand why he was not there for me to play catch, or to spend time together. He worked long hours. One thing is for sure. He was a good provider. His paychecks meant that we always had a home, nourishment, and gifts for our birthdays and Christmas.

The drive had gone by fast as I recalled those memories. I pulled into the parking garage just before it started to rain heavily. I parked in my usual spot and headed inside, down the hall and up the elevator to his room. He had been in the same room for the past few months and, even though he complained about the quality of the meals and the nurses, I still felt he was enjoying all the attention.

"Hi, Dad," I said as I entered the room.

"Hey there, where are the boys?" he asked.

He really enjoyed my children and was delighted to see them. He loved his visits with them and was very affectionate to them. He had become more talkative over the past few years and I was happy about that. It was much less awkward to sit with him for hours at a time and reflect. It was like he had all of his emotions bottled up for years and now those emotions were beginning to pour out.

"I could not bring them. The boys had tennis and a track meet," I informed him, knowing that he would be disappointed.

"Well tell them I missed them this week," he said, hoping to make me feel guilty enough to be sure they came next week.

"I will, they'll be here next weekend."

"Good, so how have you been?" he asked.

It felt so good to hear him say that. Growing up he never asked those questions. He never seemed like he really cared to ask.

"We've been good as a family," I began," but my job is really weighing me down."

"Don't worry," my dad said in complete confidence, "do you remember when I managed the furniture store and hurt my back?"

I remembered the story like it was yesterday. My father had never really asked for my help with anything. Since I was the youngest, and the only one home, he was forced to ask me for help moving some furniture in the warehouse he managed. I ended up moving a lot of furniture in a little time. He never formally thanked me for doing it, but I knew he was impressed and that was worth all of the work.

"Yes, I remember," I told him.

"At the time, I didn't want to ask for help," my dad admitted, which surprised me a little.

"Really?" I said.

"Well, you sure impressed me," he said with a laugh, "and looking back I now realize that when you're in trouble, there are people around that can help. I just didn't realize that then."

He was a hard working man who had taken on the role as the main source of income and disciplinarian for his sons. Now, those times have changed and I have picked up more roles as a father. Looking at him in his hospital bed made me realize that now it is I who had taken the responsibility as caretaker for my father and for my sons.

"Do you need anything, Dad?" I asked, as he seemed to look somewhat uncomfortable.

"Yes," he said as soon as I asked, "could you get me a pillow for my back?"

When I moved him I could tell how weak he had become. It scared me to think of him dying. We had such a close relationship now for so many years. I did not want to lose him at this time. Why did it have to be so late in life when we finally connected?

I had to keep my composure around my father and I needed to enjoy my time with him. I refused to think about what might happen in the future. It was then that I decided I would ask him a question that had been on my mind for a long time.

"Dad, if you could go back in time, would you change anything?" I asked, wondering if he had regrets.

"You know what, I would have to say no," he answered as if he had thought about it before.

A little taken aback, I turned to him and asked, "Not anything?"

"Well there are mistakes that I might avoid, but I never would do anything dramatically different. Even though I wasn't around as much as you might have liked growing up, you still turned out great. I don't think I could have done anything differently. There is nothing greater in life than seeing your son grow up and learn life's lessons. I didn't need to hand feed you your lessons. You learned those life lessons with the help of everyone around you. I'm glad you turned out so you could help an old man like me. I care about you, and I always have, I hope you know that."

It was the first time he had come out and said anything like that.

"I do know that Dad, and I'm here for you." I replied holding back my tears.

We continued on for a few hours talking about so many things. We shared memories of fishing on the river and catching so many silver bass. We talked about all his different blue collar jobs and how hard he worked at them.

While we were talking, I noticed how pale he was. He used to stand about six foot two and weigh around 220 pounds. For years I looked up to him as a giant and would always think my dad was the biggest and strongest dad around. I inherited some of those genes. I am about an inch taller and a few pounds heavier. It was difficult to see my dad in this condition and it took every ounce of me to not break down when I saw how frail he had become.

"So did you finish that article you were working on earlier?" he asked me, remembering our previous conversation.

"Yes," I started, "but it didn't turn out as well as I thought it would."

"It's Ok," he said, "you did what you could do, that's what mattered. We didn't always do everything the best way when we were in Korea, but we got the job done."
It was so strange hearing my dad talk about his war experiences. I knew that he had been a sergeant in the Marines and that he had served a full term in the Korean War, but he did not talk about those years. In these past few months he had told me war stories almost every visit.

He continued on for a few minutes about an attack they experienced and some sort of shield they had to build. Every time I heard these stories I would feel more proud to be his son. In talking with my dad about these war stories I realized how close he was to death at such an early age. Sometimes his stories would almost scare me at the thought of how close I was to never being born. It was difficult for him to be hired as an African-American man during those times. Despite any discrimination he experienced, he was able to support us and continue on.

Today when I feel discrimination I use him as a motivation to speak out against it. I attend a Catholic Church that could easily regard me as somewhat of an anomaly. I also coach tennis, a sport where African-Americans are few and far between. My attitude is like that of my father. He simply said: "that's their problem." I experienced my dad being released from jobs, but he would always cope with the situation positively and move on to his next task.

Just as I was about to go, my dad turned to me and asked, "Could you help me? I need to use the restroom."

"Sure, Dad," I replied as I picked him up.

He was so light. I could not believe how much weight he had lost. I carried him in my arms like he was a child. As we were walking back it was a tender moment. He laid his head on my shoulder gently and sighed. It felt so comfortable to hold my father in my arms. As he rested there, seeming so peaceful, he took his hand and placed it on my cheek. Never had his touch felt so warm and so caring. He put his hand on my face and looked up at me and said, "I love you, Son."

"I love you too, Dad," I said as a tear rolled down my face.

My dad's failing body was relying solely on my strength. I laid him in his bed and I could tell he was getting tired. I do not think he even realized how important a moment we had just shared. I doubt he even knew how much it meant for me to see him every week in the hospital.

Many of these realizations about him have come to me very late in life. Even today I continue to think about my father and change my parenting styles based on what he taught me. Even though he did not spend much time with me playing sports or going to my games, I know that he still cared and wanted to be there. Today, I am active in my sons' lives and want to continue to be throughout their adulthood.

My father and I bonded and shared our emotions very late in his life. I am thankful that I was able to spend those last few months with him the way I did. Those visits to the hospital and the sharing of memories made it much easier for me to deal with his death. I could not imagine that he would have died without talking about so many of those memories that could have been lost forever.

I continue to realize how important the father and son relationship is, and I value every moment I share with my two sons. I see them developing into adults and I see them maturing into great individuals. I look at them and I feel the same way my dad said he felt about me. He told me that he would not do anything differently. I feel the exact same way today. I hope that one day when I am much older my children will be there taking care of me. Until then, I will live my life like my father, with no excuses and no regrets.

The Son
A lesson from the coach...

"But, Dad, I've been doing everything you told me. He's not that much better than me." I was over at the fence talking to my dad between points.

"Listen," my dad began to explain again, "all you have to do is work hard to finish those points. You are just being lazy with your shots."

Usually a son would not be too happy with his dad if he told him that he was being lazy in a match, but when he has been your tennis coach for the past seven years, you need to listen. We were in the middle of one of the most important matches of the summer. The boy I challenged was my age and he had been in the same tennis class for the past five years. He was a strong player, but I should have been able to defeat him. Yet, I could not even win one game against him.

The match took over an hour and a half to play, but the score did not show how hard it had been. I had lost the match 6-0, 6-0 and I was absolutely devastated. I knew that my father was disappointed as well. He had always taken how I had developed my talents very seriously.

"Dad," I said as we were getting in the car, "I don't think I could have played any worse today."

If I thought he would say that I did fine and I did my best, I was about to be disappointed.

"No, I don't think you could have," he immediately responded.

I was a little surprised at those candid words.

Although I felt like I deserved it, I was still shocked. I had just lost in the second round of a tournament for which I had been preparing for a long time.

"Where are we going?" I asked finally breaking the silence of a ride.

"You'll see," my dad said, "it will be a surprise."

It was one of Dad's surprises. It would either be something extremely good and enjoyable or maybe an exciting adventure. As we turned the corner I still had no idea where we were going. Dad always liked to surprise me.

"At least give me a clue," I told him as we headed into the city.

"We haven't been there in a while and we really need to go," he said in a stern voice.

At that time I figured we were going to the club where I started playing tennis. He might have called my old coach from whom I first learned to play. All of a sudden we just pulled over in the middle of Main Street. Startled, I quickly turned to my dad and smiled. We were going to the bookstore! I could not believe it. I had not bought a new book in ages.

"I figured we needed a break from tennis," he said as we came to a stop.

These trips to the bookstore used to be our favorite thing to do together. We usually would go for hours and look through all the new titles. My dad had always been a strong believer in having reading materials around the house. Ever since I was young, he had taught me the importance of reading and how to choose a book that I would truly enjoy.

We strolled up and down the aisles together looking through the shelves of old and new books. Occasionally my dad would pick up one and start looking through it and tell me of the books he used to read when he was younger. The best part about going to the bookstore with him was that he enjoyed it just as much as I. Although he was my tennis coach and a demanding father at home as well, he definitely let me see the lighter side of him quite often.

"Dad, look at this history series. Do you remember when I first got it?"

I remembered it like it was yesterday. We were visiting the store for the first time together. He had been stressed at work and my mom and he were in a little argument about something of little importance. He really wanted to get out of the house, so he took me to the store. I remember sitting on his lap reading the entire book to him. Even though it took me almost an hour to get through an entire text, he sat there with such patience to help me through the reading.

"Of course I do, it was your first book," Dad said as he looked through it.

"Listen," he began, "don't worry about your match today, I know you're a great player and will do fine next time. You just didn't try your hardest today."
Even though I had temporarily forgotten about the match already I replied and told him, "I know, I know. It's just

that it seems so hard sometimes."

"It doesn't matter how hard something is. Anyone has the power to do it if they try hard enough," he explained.

"I know, but with school and everything else I don't think I have the skill and time to get it all done."

"It may seem hard now, but you'll see in a few years that these years of your life were a good time."

It was not only the match. I had received a poor report card the previous semester and my parents were disappointed. I was even more disappointed in myself.

"In school, anything is possible with effort," he continued to explain.

"I know, but it just seems so hard, no one did that well in those classes."

"It doesn't matter what others do," he continued with his lecture, "you can still do it."

I had heard this lecture a million times. He always said that you can do anything if you put in the effort. I agreed with him, but it just seemed like it did not apply to me. I did not want to talk about school at that point so I quickly shifted the conversation back to the books.
"Did you ever read this one?" I asked him as I held it up, hoping to change the topic. I looked up at my dad and I was glad we were spending this time together. I had never thought this day was going to turn out like this. It started early in the morning with a long heated tennis match. It ended in that store with what would become a second home to us over the years.

While we were looking through another shelf of older books my dad turned to me and said, "This one reminds me of when I was your age."

He never really told me much about when he was a child, so I turned to him with genuine interest and asked, "What about when you were my age?"

"It was just the same problems as you. I was a struggling inner-city boy with a lot of responsibilities. I was the youngest of all my friends and I was on my own. Even though I didn't play tennis, I played other sports and I was easily distracted."

"But you did fine in school. You were nothing like me."

"Now I wouldn't go around saying that. Did you know that when I was in the eighth grade I failed four classes?"

"Really," I asked very surprised, "I thought you had good grades."

"Well I did eventually," he started to say, "I did horribly my eighth grade year and my first year in high school. I was almost kicked out of school. Then all of a sudden I realized that I needed to be getting a good education. My dad sat me down and told me that I needed to pull my act together. And I did. I went on and never received any grade lower than a B. I eventually did even better and became valedictorian of my class even after that terrible start. It just proves that you can do it."

"But that was you, it's not me," I admitted.

"You are smarter than I was. Your marks this first year were much better than mine. You're just getting started. If you work at it you could be more successful than I was."

The more I thought about it, the more I might have been wrong. There were times when I could have studied more and not played video games. Even though I did not want to admit it, Dad was right.

"Look at this book here." my dad remarked. "Even though it is made up and unrealistic, you can still see how hard work pays off. In so many stories all of the heroes had struggles and they had to overcome their doubts. You have a struggle now and I know you have the power in you to become that hero."

As simple as that was, it gave me a little motivation.

"Thanks Dad," I said as I sat down next to him, "I know I can work harder."

My dad had always told me about struggles and how he had made it through. He had told me how hard it could be to be a black man in this country. He had told me a few stories about his dad and how he was a war hero in the Korean War.

We realized that we had been there a little too long and probably should get back for dinner. On the way out he surprised me with a few new books.

"Dad," I said when we got into the car, "thanks for this afternoon, I needed that."

"I figured you did," he replied with a smile. "After a massacre like that anyone would need a break."

I hoped that my mom would make my favorite dinner due to the circumstances. When I walked in my mom hugged me as a sign of her support.

"I'm cooking something special for dinner," she informed me with one of her smiles.

I walked through the kitchen and looked in the oven to see my mom's lasagna. She did not make it often, but this was one of those times I needed it. It felt good knowing that everyone cared so much.

We had a great dinner that helped put the morning's match behind me. Soon after we were finished I found myself with my dad in the living room. It had been a very special day with him.

"You know that even though you lost today, you're still a heck of a tennis player."

"Thanks Dad," I replied.

"And don't worry about school either," he continued, "you're very smart, you'll figure everything out."

"I know," I said looking down at the ground embarrassed that I even brought up my struggles knowing what he had been through, "Things will improve!"

"They had better," my dad said jokingly, "or I'm going to have to open up a credit line at the bookstore!"

As I read about all of the different heroes and their struggles, I could not help but put myself in their situations. Every time they encounter an evil villain I looked at it like a test or a match. When I finished the chapter I got up and was headed to bed. Every night my dad and mom would always tell me they loved me and I would tell them that I loved them as well. As I walked out of the room I heard my dad call my name.

"Mikey," he said, "I love you."

"I love you too, Dad," I said as I turned to go up-stairs.

As I lay in bed that night I was taking everything in. Even though it was a bad tennis match, I knew that it would eventually make me stronger. While listening to my dad I realized the problems I have aren't nearly as bad as they could be. That day I think I had grown up a notch thanks to my father and the boy inside of him.

The bookstore would always be a safe haven. Even today, three years later, we still visit it from time to time. It is an escape for both of us. We are able to spend time together and enjoy our favorite hobby. Dad has taught me that with effort I can achieve anything. My father is my hero. For me, he will always be the greatest hero of all.

Dad, Farm, Family

A son's life in the country is tied to the family farm and that country earth provides a place where hard work binds family together. Even as a son leaves home to create a new life, the lessons of family carry on within him. A new generation soon benefits from those lessons. In an age where many farms have seemed to succumb to urban centers, it is good to know the strong family work ethic can still be transmitted from father to son. The rural environment has something to teach us about our fathers and about our families.

The Father
I learned the lessons of family...

The memories of my father are few and limited in number. My best recollections of him are seeing him on our family farm over forty years ago. I spent my childhood in southern Ohio. Every morning was the same routine. We woke up at the crack of dawn to do our chores. The children all slept in the same room of that country house and we learned to develop our morning ritual so that all of us were up and ready on time for the work that had to be done.

"Time to get up," my dad said as he opened up the door early that Saturday morning.

It was odd how we would do chores for hours upon hours with no complaining. I am not sure whether it was because it was a sense of duty, or it was how we were raised, or because we knew no other way.

"You all sleep well last night?" he asked us as we scurried around the room getting dressed.

There was something about getting up on the weekends that was extra hard. I imagined city people had the luxury of sleeping in on weekends. Our lives were good and we all worked together as a family. I think my dad enjoyed that the most. He was assuredly the most enthusiastic about it.

After we did our first couple chores, we went in to eat. My mom usually would make us a good breakfast. That was the advantage of living on a farm. We always had eggs and milk. A good homemade breakfast was standard.

"Are you boys going to work on the new fence today?" my mom asked as we passed the food around the table.

"I think Bill and I will finish it today," I told her confidently.

As I reflect upon all the tasks we had to do those years, I realize how much freedom and responsibility Dad gave us. We had been on tractors since we were six years old. I had my own tractor since I was eight. We were all energetic and that made the farm very productive. It may have seemed like we did a lot of the farming, but the true brains of the operation was Dad. He radiated with farm knowledge and we learned our trade from him. There was not a single job on that farm that he was unable to do.

After breakfast we headed out into the fields. It was late in the summer and there was much to be done. We each climbed up on our tractors and rode out to our tasks. During the morning hours we did not see much of each other. Between breakfast and lunch we would usually be about our individual responsibilities. I did not complain as it was a great time to be alone and close to the earth. On that particular day I was thinking about my dad more than usual. Every morning he assigned the chores, but he not only supervised our work, he did a lion's share himself. He was accustomed to carrying out tasks successfully and he had learned that expertise as a soldier in World War II. His dream as he served in the war was to return home, buy a farm and live there for the rest of his life. That is what he did and that is what he loved.

As I came around the last turn I saw my dad by the cattle fence waving me over. I headed in that direction and pulled up next to him.

"What's going on, Dad?" I asked as he finished fixing some wire on the fence.

"Are you boys going to finish that fence?" he asked, expecting the affirmative.

"Yes Dad, we will finish it today."

"Good," he said, "because I need it finished before we get the hogs next week."

"Alright then, I'll get back to work," I said.

He may have seemed to be an abrupt man who didn't show many emotions, but I knew his other side. He was a much different man during Thanksgiving or Christmas or when his brothers and the rest of our family would visit. On those occasions he would seem to relax, smile more, and not be so anxious to finish a task. The past year he had invited me on one of his hunting trips. It was another occasion to see my dad relaxed and enjoying himself without the worries of the farm on his mind. I felt that I understood him better through those special occasions.

That year I wanted to go to college and I knew that he would help me in any way he could. I was feeling the pull between responsibility for the farm and my desire to finish my education. One afternoon I expressed to my father my hope for more schooling and his response encouraged me.

"We'll make it work," he told me. "I want as many of you as possible to have that opportunity."

That made me even more eager to finish the fence. Sometimes we had to bail hay or even more difficult, help my dad fix the tractors. Even if it seemed there was nothing else to do, my dad would always find something. I was fortunate on that day that our main task was repairing that fence.

"You think we'll finish this today?" I asked my older brother as we were hammering the stakes into the ground.

"I hope so," he said, "Dad wants it finished by today. Even Mom mentioned it."

"Yeah," I said looking around, "but we have a lot more to do."

"Dad is bound to be out here soon," my brother said, "but I hope we will be able to finish this ourselves."

All of us wanted to do what pleased him. We wanted him to know we would do a job successfully.

We continued to work into the hot hours of the afternoon. We still had to go back into the fields before it was dark, so we were really trying to finish this job quickly. As we were hammering the last stake into the ground my dad came over to us.

"You guys need help with that?" he asked in a surprisingly enthusiastic tone.

"We are almost done, Dad," I said, not wanting to completely admit we needed help.

"Ok," he said, "when I finish up in the next field I'll be back over."

Fifteen minutes later my dad made his way back over to the fence. It had been a simple project although tedious. As we finished, Dad started to talk to us. We usually did not talk when he was around because he was usually assigning the tasks and explaining the best method to do the job that was required.

"You boys have these stakes in here pretty good," he said, complimenting us.

"We did what you told us," my brother said, not taking any of the credit.

"Do you want to go out for dinner tonight?" he asked as he was wrapping the wire around one of the stakes.

"Yes," my brother and I said almost in unison.

We rarely went out to eat as a family. Such dinners were usually out of the ordinary unless there was a particular reason to celebrate. We had worked harder than usual that week and the farm was in good shape. This could have been his reward to us for a job well done. We usually had a traditional dinner where everyone was expected to be present. Rarely did we have friends over or did we have time to go somewhere else. I'm not sure who enforced the dinner rule more, my mother or my father, but we always were expected to be there together.

To most people this day looks like an average day for a farm boy. In many ways, that is true. The memories of my dad surround the simple things, and a simple life. I cannot remember many deep conversations or life shattering experiences. We spent those years on the farm, working side by side with him and the rest of my family. I learned the lessons of family for use in the years to come.

Today, even though I am not the same person my father was, I work very hard like him to support my family. I also reward them when they do good work and I love them just as much as my father loved me. Others may have seen his reserved, distant side, but he was a warm and loving father to me. His small smiles at the dinner table and his occasional surprises left me knowing that he did care. To this day, whenever anyone should ask what the word father means for me, I look back on what was best about Dad, the farm and our lives together.

The Son

Learning at the home game...

It was my freshmen year and I was finally able to show my father around the campus and take him to a game when his favorite team was in town.

"They're not going to stand a chance," I told my dad as we were driving to the game.

"We'll see," my dad said, not ready to argue the point, just hinting at the fact that one never really knows for sure.

"Michigan is so much better this year," I continued. "We are going to win by at least twenty."

"Well we'll just have to wait and see," my dad said.
I had been rubbing it in all week and he would not say anything at all. It was good that we had something to distract us from what had just happened. A few weeks earlier my dad had lost his mother and he was still in the grieving process. Football conversation was one way out for him.

"So how do you like the games?" he asked as we pulled into a parking space.

"They're great," I said, "There's nothing like a game at the Big House!"

He was very non-judgmental about my going to the University of Michigan even though he was a fan of Ohio State. He had gone to college in Ohio and had loved his experience there. I was an engineering major, so I chose to go through this engineering school. That was not the issue now. This Saturday it was all about one of the biggest rivalries in college football.

We found a parking space within a mile of the stadium, parked the car and began walking. I was wearing blue and my dad was wearing red. Being a fan for an opposing team could be quite intimidating and even dangerous!

"Hey, loser!" a Michigan fan yelled as we were walking by.

We entered the gates of the stadium; we had tickets near the student section. The remarks continued and actually got even worse. As he was the only opposing team fan in the entire section, it must have been difficult for him. He remained calm and seemed to prepare himself for the energy of the game.

It was a close game but this time the outcome was not good for Michigan. I had cheered with the man fans who would say something to him like, "Uh-oh, looks like all that maize and blue was too much for them." He would just sit there and smile saying, "We'll see."

We lost the game. He did not say a word about it. If we would have won, he would not have heard the end of it from me until the next year. He just sat there in a calm way and said it was a great game. There was not a hint of sarcasm in his voice.

"What a great game!" he said again as we walked back to the car.

"It was a good game," I admitted even though I was still disappointed.

My dad had never been one to rub things in or even talk about things like that very often. He was a very loving father and even though we had been distant over the past few years he still showed he cared. By going to the home game with me I realized that he wanted to spend time with me. Even though he knew that it would be uncomfortable to be an opposing fan in that stadium, he still was willing to be there and to spend time with me.

After the game we headed back home for the rest of the weekend. Mom was happy to see me and I was happy to be home. Even though the university was only about an hour and a half from our house, I did not make it home very often that first semester. We had planned a trip the next day back to southern Ohio to sort through my grandmother's effects. Nobody was looking forward to that job, but we knew it had to be done.

The next morning Mom told us that she was not going to be able to make the trip. It was a drive lasting almost three and a half hours, but I knew she probably had a reason. I really did not want to go on the trip either and hoped that my dad would decide to go alone.

"I think this will be a good opportunity for you to be with your dad," Mom told me.

I decided that she was probably right and so I went to bed early that night. That morning we got an early start and we were on the road by 6:30.

"So how's school going?" my dad asked ending the silence between us.

"It's going good," I stated, "the class work is a lot harder than I'm used to."

"Yes, I remember my first years of school," he said, showing signs of opening up.

It was the first time he had even mentioned anything about his past. The only things I knew about him were the stories that Grandma used to tell, but now that she was gone, the mystery of his past would have to remain a mystery.

"It was tough leaving the farm," Dad started, "we worked hard together and there was still a lot to do. A few of my brothers stayed around, but I really wanted to go to college. It was my dad who let me go."

The only thing I knew about my grandfather was that he was a strict farmer who demanded many long hours of work from his sons. I had been under the impression that my father did not like his dad very much. Now he was telling me it was tough leaving him.

"Really?" I asked in complete surprise. "I thought you didn't like your dad!"

"No, no," he started to explain, "I liked my dad. He just never really showed others that he cared very much. He was a great man and had a very fulfilling life. I hope to do as well."

"But didn't he just work all day, every day on a farm?" I asked looking out the window at all the farm country as we passed.

"He did work a lot, yes," Dad explained. "But he enjoyed what he did and he wouldn't have lived his life any other way."

"What was he like?" I asked, thinking that I really did not know much about him.

"Well," he started, "He was quiet and very strict. The only time he ever opened his mouth was basically to give instructions or scold us. He had other ways of showing that he cared."

I was not sure he knew how much he was like his dad. He also had been strict with us for as long as we can remember. I rarely spent time with him during my high school years. When I was a child, he had left for almost twelve months to live and work in France. I remember the calls he made to my mother and the occasional word he would say to each of us as we shared the phone.

"What was your dad like before he got the farm?" I asked, taking advantage of this rare opportunity to share in some of his memories.

"Well, he drove tractors in the Philippines during World War II. He met your grandmother when he returned and they were married. They bought a farm not long after. That's pretty much all I know."

"Did you ever talk to him about anything in his past?" I asked.

"No, we rarely talked. The only time I remember doing any talking was at the holidays."

The memories continued to flow out. I found out so much more about my dad and his family. He told me about his brothers and the memories of what they did together on the farm. He talked about the games they played, the trouble they got into, and many other family events. Knowing about my dad's past helped us grow together as father and son.

That morning we talked for three and a half hours. I think we talked more in that car than we had in the entire past year. That afternoon was an interesting experience as we sorted through all of my grandmother's old things as he and his brothers looked through the family treasures. The artifacts brought back many more memories for them.

My father was there to support everyone, and it was obvious that he was an important part of the family. On the way home I took the opportunity to ask him about the experience of losing his mom and reuniting with his brothers.

"Dad, how come you don't show emotion that much?' I asked, amazing myself that I would even ask such a question.

"Well, I just don't see the point," he began to explain, "I accept what life gives me and I don't feel like I need to do anything else."

"I guess so," I said, "but even at the game you could have really taken advantage of our loss. You could have got back at the people who were mean to you."

"I know I could have done that. But again, there's no point. I know that you were upset with the game. Why would I want to make it worse for you?"

I never heard him complain about anything. Ever since I can remember he had never talked about his work or anything that surrounds it. It was amazing how much my dad was like his father!

We talked more about his past and even my future. I was excited to go into the engineering field. My dad received his degree in engineering as well. I was proud to follow in his footsteps. As he talked about his relationship with his dad, I saw that there were many similarities in our relationship.

That was a trip I was glad we made. I learned that it is important to keep a family connection, that the country would always be my heritage, and that my father was my role model.

Life Lasting Impressions

Sons are impressionable and fathers can make a deep impression. When fathers are able to take time from the work that has to be done to bond with their sons, a new relationship begins. Fathers and sons deepen their understanding and remember it for a lifetime. The good father will set aside his plans and his work on many occasions to meet the expectations and hopes of his son. When he is able to do this he makes a lasting impression. These sons needed such signs of affection and attention. They learned to return them and to be free to give affection to others as well.

The Father
I saw his other side...

Rain always made the day go by slowly. It seemed like it had been raining forever. It was spring and there was only a month and a half of school before the summer break. My brothers and I did not have much to do when we returned home from school.

"I'm sick of doing homework," I told my brother John as we sat there at the kitchen table on that cold rainy night.

We were a lower middle class family growing up in a small city. Most of the memories I have of childhood involve playing in the street with other boys in our neighborhood.

My dad was a very focused man. He was a hard working accountant laboring fifty-five to sixty hours per week. He worked for a firm during the day and would spend every night and some of the weekend working on tax returns. He was unable to have much quality time with us, yet one of the clear memories I have of my father was on this cold and rainy night.

We sat at dinner talking with my mother. Occasionally my dad would inject his opinion. He did not appear to care as much about the other activities in our lives as he did about our education.

"Why are you getting such low marks?" he would ask regarding our grades.

"Because it's a hard class and I have practice all the time, so I don't have time to study."

"That's not an excuse," he said. "I know you can do better."

Dad once had tuberculosis and he had been in the hospital a total of three years during my childhood. His health had diminished over the past few years and he seemed to become more involved in his work.

The next day we were all outside playing with my sister and brother when we decided to go for a walk. As we were leaving, my dad walked out to join us. Usually when we walked we would go down to the junior high school. It was not a play area for other young people in our neighborhood. Usually there was just our family and a few close friends. During that walk I took the opportunity to look at my dad. I did not understand him. If he was trying to be closer to us, why did he not say anything or do anything? I am sure that my brother and sister were thinking the same thing because nobody dared to break the silence. Just when we started to head back, my brother suggested that we should race.

"Come on," he said, "I'll race you guys to the end of the street."

"OK," my sister and I said.

So we all lined up waiting.

"On your mark, get set," my brother began.

I remember my dad crouching down and getting into a runner's block start. He was actually going to race with us.

His lungs were not in good shape and he probably should not have been doing this.

"Go!" my brother yelled.

Something terrible happened. My dad slipped on the pavement and hit his face shattering his glasses. It was an awkward fall and his head was bleeding. The amount of blood made the situation seem frantic. I pulled off my shirt, held it against his face and stayed with him as my brother and sister ran to get help.

It was not long until my mother arrived and drove Dad to the emergency room. He needed six stitches on his face and he was shaken up, but the doctors reported that he would recover quickly. It was unfortunate that one of the few times my dad tried to do something with us he had to suffer this in doing so.

A few weeks passed and he made a full recovery. The race we started together, although it had a horrible outcome, helped me see a new side of my father. He showed that he did care about us enough to join in our activities.

Another experience I vividly remember occurred one night as we were sitting around the table eating dinner. A sudden announcement was made concerning breaking news. We were all talking when suddenly both my parents went silent. It took me a few moments to realize what was going on, but I soon understood that they were shocked by a news report from the television.

"A tragic accident that one can never comprehend," the news reporter began to say, "a day like any other has turned into devastation for a group of small children."

It was a horrible story. There had been a fire in a school and a group of children and their teachers were burned to death. It was so tragic that I knew my mother would be deeply affected. I looked at her and she was dabbing at her eyes. But then, on the opposite side of the table, I saw something I never expected to see. My dad was also deeply moved and the tears were also welling up in his eyes. He was not an overtly religious man, and he never acted like he could be affected by such a story. To this day, just thinking of my father crying rouses emotion in me. Seeing a man who was such a strong authoritative figure in my life cry in front of me is an event that is hard to forget.

"Honey, are you Ok?" my mom asked him.

He did not respond. I do not think he wanted to say anything in front of us. This vulnerable side of my father was attractive to me. Later that night we were watching television as a family. As I sat there in the dark, I found myself thinking that Dad had become a different man. His health had not been the greatest the past ten years. I looked at him in the dim light through the flicker of the television screen, and at that moment I realized how much I admired him.

When the time came for me to go to college, he was there to support me in that decision. His actions as a father answered my needs and often resolved our little problems.

Today my children are my world and I let them know it every day of their lives. My son and I are the best of friends. I look forward to the upcoming birth of my grandchild. I have tried to help my children with all their little problems. Those two days when my father showed me his true feelings are the days I remember him truly being 'my dad.' I have made it a goal in my life to be sure that they feel that way. I show them how much I care and constantly try to be an active part in their lives.

Although my father and I differ in so many ways in our lives, I still value those memories. He may have not even realized the lessons he passed on to me or what I thought about him as a father. If he were around today I would be anxious to talk to him about my children and grandchildren. I think every father instills life-lasting impressions on his children. I was impressed by my Dad. I want my children to receive the benefits that can be theirs as they attempt to understand the man who is their father.

The Son

Hugs were a way of life...

"Bye, Dad," I said as I started walking away from the car where he stood.

"Come here," he said, "I need a hug."

I knew it was impossible to get out of it. I did not mind at all. We have always been a very affectionate father and son. So I went over to him and gave him a big hug before I headed off to school.

"I hope I can always hug you like this and you will never care," he said.

"What are you talking about?" I asked, having no idea.

"You'll understand someday," he said as he squeezed me one last time.

And he was right. Being only nine years old at the time, I had no idea to what he referred. Our family has always hugged and it was not until my middle school years that I would realize how much love were in those hugs.

My father and I have always had a strong relationship. Ever since I can remember he has told me he loved me on a daily basis. For most sons that changes through high school, but not in my house. We were always welcome to show emotion and affection and we were never afraid at all. The hug he gave me in the third grade was a hug that would continue for an entire lifetime.

Dad spent many hours with me in those years. We were involved in a weekly Indian Guide group. The group was meeting at my friend's house and I had been looking forward to the pumpkin carving for Halloween.

"You ready to go?" I asked as I waited at the door.

"Yes, just let me get the carving supplies," he said as he hurried around in the kitchen.

He was always trying to please us. We were not spoiled in the material sense of the word, but he always wanted us to be happy. We would play games, go for walks, anything we could possibly do together to spend time.

"You know," he said, "I really like going to these Indian Guide groups with you."

"Me too," I said as he put his arm around me.

"There they are!" the group leader yelled out as we walked through the fence into my friend's backyard.

"Let's get carving," my dad said.

That entire afternoon we spent together carving pumpkins and talking with the other fathers and sons. My dad was such a social guy he was always able to make conversation with the people around us. I did not understand it at the time, but now I see how positive he was about life. The reason for that positive outlook would be made known to me that very night.

"How does that look?" I asked him as I had carved my first pumpkin by myself.

"That looks good. How's mine?" he asked as he held up the ugliest looking pumpkin I had ever seen.

"It needs a little work I think," I said, as we both laughed.

These Indian Guide groups were indeed fun. Even though we stopped going a few years later, we continued to get together on the weekends and we still called it our 'Guide group,' even though it was just the two of us.

After we finished carving the pumpkins we ate dinner together. Usually the host family for the week would provide the main dish and the guests would bring side dishes. It was another way for everyone to spend time with their dads.

"Who are you trick-or-treating with this year?" my dad asked as we sat down to eat.

"I don't know," I told him. "All my friends are just hanging out at one house and aren't going to trick-or-treat that much."

"Well you don't have to do that," my dad explained. "You could have a couple of friends over to our house and you could trick-or-treat in our neighborhood."

"I guess we could do that," I said in a half-hearted voice.

After dinner we walked home together. The activities the group provided always encouraged the fathers and sons to communicate and do things together. I think it was fortunate that we had such a group for that purpose.

That night we sat together as a family and watched television. I remember that Dad left us to go upstairs. I followed him to see what he was doing. He sat on his bed and got out a pocket book and a pen.

"What are you doing up here, Dad? I asked as I sat on his bed next to him.

"Oh, nothing," he said as he began writing.

"What are you writing? Are you working?"

"No, No," he began to explain. "This is just something that helps me be positive."

"What do you do?" I asked

"It's actually simple. I call it my good book. Each day I look at everything that I did during the day. I look at everything that gave me a good feeling or something good I want to remember. I have been doing this ever since I was in college."

"What are you writing about today?"

He had written three memories of the day:

1. I met a fine man at the Indian Guide group and he gave me a compliment about my shirt.

2. My son and I had a laugh together while we were carving our pumpkins.

3. I love my son and I am proud of him.

"I love you too dad," I told him as we hugged, "Thanks."

Most of his notes had to do with work and other little things, but my name was there quite often. It was such a great feeling to know my dad felt that way. It was not that I never heard that he loved me and that he was proud of me, as much as the fact that he had written it in his book. This meant that not only did he say that to me but he was thinking it on a daily basis.

The relationship my dad built for us has lasted a lifetime. Now that I am expecting a child of my own I will remember the things my father did for me while I was growing up. Even though I do not actually write them in a book, I think a valuable lesson can be drawn from such a journal. The key to his success was his positive approach to life. I never heard him complain about work or complain about anything to my mother. He might have had the worst day in the world, but when he saw my sister and me, he would not let his bad day affect ours.

Today, I still value my father's relationship and we are in communication at least once or twice a week. We live about an hour away from each other, which is the farthest I have ever been from him. Not a day goes by when I do not think of my dad and all that he has done for me. I am anticipating the joy I will feel to show him his first grandchild.

The good book that my father used will always be a memory and a source of inspiration for me. I will remember that staying positive can make a world of difference for my child as surely as it has made a world of difference for my father and me.

Seven Is Our Lucky Number

This father and son both came from a family of seven children. They learned that simple joys can be the wonderful experiences of life that overcome the hard times. True wealth and true security could not be measured in dollars. These two loving, caring fathers knew that as they showered attention on their children they minimized the uncertainty and doubt that an unknown future provided. Good fathers teach their sons to trust, not only in them, but in others. Then sons can learn to trust themselves.

The Father

Lessons in driving...

"Always give the other guy a way out. Be a gentleman."

That is what my father taught me in those early years when I used to watch him carefully. Our relationship was one of example. I just believed that if I watched and did what my dad did, I could not go wrong. He seemed to always do the best he could at anything he was doing. He was focused, and the task before him seemed so clear.

"Do the best you can. It may not be done perfectly, but do not let that stop you from doing your best!"

I remember being in the front seat of the car with my dad once when I obviously noticed something in the road before he did. "Dad, look out!" I screamed. A dog was lying there and it just was too late to swerve and miss it. The thud was unmistakably painful and the rear wheels hit it again, only increasing that sick feeling in my stomach. My father pulled the car over to the side and was visibly shaken and breathing heavily.

"It was a dog," I said, somehow feeling the need to explain in case he may not have realized it.

"I know, I know," he repeated, "it came up so fast! Was it moving?"

I immediately looked back to the scene to note that there was no movement now.

"I think he is dead Dad," I sadly announced.

His did not receive that news well. He was never one to neglect the responsibility for his actions, but I had never seen him this distressed.

"I've seen animals suffer. I hate that. Get that blanket from the trunk."

I opened the hatch and pulled out an old blanket he kept there and followed him back to where the dog lay motionless at the side of the road. He noted and told me that there was no collar or name and then he carefully wrapped the animal and carried it in his arms back to our car.

"Do you want me to open the trunk?" I asked.

"No, let's place him in the rear seat," he answered.

He gently laid the dog there and then we both got in the front seat.

"Where are we going to take him, Dad?" I said as we drove off.

"Home is the place. We will bury him there. It's the best we can do for him."

I knew my father would never fail from doing what he felt was the best he could in any situation that arose. I wanted to be that kind of man as well, focused in what I was doing and an example for my children.

I remember when I was sixteen and I proudly received my driver's license. I had spent months studying the rules and regulations, preparing for that driver's test and promising to take the obligation of driving seriously. I did not know how my father would respond to another driver in the house. I knew that I had done my best and I wanted him to know about it. He came home early that day and immediately called me into the front room of the house. I was expecting a lecture on responsibility, but instead I was greeted with a broad smile and a hand held up holding the car keys.

"I'm really impressed," he said, "It's time for you to go impress your friends!" He slapped the keys firmly in my hand, and did not even wait for my reaction. He left the room and headed upstairs. It was one of those manhood moments that I will never forget. My dad was proud of me and he completely trusted me. I was now a little more independent in my eyes and a little more mature in his. I enthusiastically rushed out the door, and then quickly composed myself for the confident strut to the car; soon to be all mine as I drove into town. I did not want to look back at the house. Maybe Dad was watching from his window to see how I would react. I wanted him to know that I would be careful and that I would be doing my best.

I reflect upon these experiences with Dad now that I have seven children of my own. Since our marriage, my wife and I had always feared the day would come. And now it was here. Our oldest was of age and was standing before me with the request that would send chills down my spine.

"I'm old enough to drive now, Dad, can you teach me? Mom doesn't need the car today!" I just was not ready for that request, or maybe it was that I just did not want to accept all those years had passed since my father had trusted me. Was it not just a few years since we had struggled together to learn to ride that bicycle? What would dad do in my place? What a shame that he had died the very year my first son was born. He never would know him. I wanted so much to present him with a grandson, and I wanted my son to know how wise a man I had for a father. Now he just stood there looking at me and waiting for the response I would give.

"Do you think you are ready for that?" I asked, immediately realizing my mistake as his face dropped in disappointment.

"Are you free for the afternoon?" I recovered.

"Yes, Dad. Ready and willing!" He breathed easier.

"Let's tell your mother we will be gone for a while."

He was gone, off to do that duty before I had finished speaking. Within a minute her face appeared around the corner with that "better you than me" look she always gave in such situations, and I had to smile at her to prop her up.

"We're going driving," I said. I tried to make it one of those father-son bonding events that she had so encouraged me to do in the past. The reference did not pass her by without a comment.

"Well, don't let anything stop you from doing your best!" she said with a smirk on her face. She knew all my stories and she never failed to hold me accountable for them.

Now I was really under pressure. I had to live up to my father's example. It was time to ignore my formal education! My wife watched us drive off until we were out of sight.

I admit that I was a little nervous to take on the role of driving instructor. I was somewhere between thinking there are already too many young and inexperienced drivers on the roads and being guilty of my own inadequacy. My son held tight to the steering wheel, seeming to hope that no other cars would appear on the road ahead.

"Relax," I said, realizing how ridiculous a command that was.

"I'm Ok," he responded in frustration, as he panned the road ahead daring a vehicle to appear.

"Make a left at the next corner," I commanded in my best instructive voice.

He slowed down, signaled and negotiated the turn perfectly.

"Great job," I told him. "Now let's go down to the park and we can practice some parallel parking."

He nodded, keeping his eyes fixed on the road, still with an air of defiance that made me glad I was not in an opposing car. The smile quickly left my face as he slammed on the brakes and came to a halt for what I thought was no apparent reason.

"What's the matter?" I bellowed.

"Didn't you see him, Dad?"

"No, see what?"

He jumped out of the car and disappeared in front of the hood. Smiling, he rose, cradling in his arms the mangiest mutt I had ever seen!

"You didn't hit him, did you? " I asked.

"No Dad, I missed him by at least a foot," he smiled.

There was no identification, no particular markings, and no handsome profile that would find this stray a home.

"Well, let's take him home," I heard myself saying, even though I knew my wife would be my next obstacle.

"Can you drive, Dad?" he asked as he cradled the sorriest expression I had ever seen on a dog's face. "If I keep holding him he won't be afraid."

Well, we did end up keeping that dog, in spite of those looks I received from my wife.

"I thought this was supposed to be a driving lesson," she noted with candor.

"I just could not leave him in the road," I responded. "What would you have me do?"

"Your best," she retorted, making those annoying click-ing noises only wives can do so well as she walked down the hall toward our bedroom.

I did not have to have seven children. It was not like I had to do everything my father did to prove to him that I was a success! That is fourteen little eyes looking at you, fourteen little legs running in every direction, fourteen lit-tle arms holding onto you in times of trouble. Yet, that was exactly what I did.

I wanted to be the type of father that taught my children by example, a mentor, a leader. A father who would call them to excellence, yet be forgiving, and doing it all with a sense of humor. Was that to much to achieve? My father seemed to take it all in stride.

The Great Depression hit my father's family hard. Like many other sons of the age, education had to be put aside when the opportunity of a job arose, as the support it would bring to the family seemed paramount. These may have been hard times, but they also had benefits. The fam-ily unit seemed to have more importance and receive more emphasis. Young men grew up fast. Formal education was often replaced with life's experiences. Growing up in my father's home, I never thought that his lack of education prevented him from excelling. I remember thinking that he was such a smart man. He was insatiably curious about things. Whenever a new product or piece of furniture came into our home, he would check into how it was construct-ed, sometimes even taking it apart to examine the inner workings. That curiosity was certainly passed on to me, the eldest of his seven children. Although I did not experi-ence the Depression, there were those hard times in my life which indeed paralleled my dad's experiences. It is that same discipline I see reflected in my life that I hoped I would pass on to my seven children.

Like him, I moved from job to job throughout my career. I think I was just as inquisitive, just as curious, and never satisfied with the same old routine. I traveled around the country in many different jobs. Those fourteen eyes kept watching me carefully as we traveled.

When I think of my father I remember a wise man who taught me what it meant to be a gentleman. It was a time of discipline then. I think that was good, and I am the better for it. I really learned the most from him as he took on the role of mentor. It was in these times that my eyes would grow larger as I watched and learned from his example. He could be firm yet at the same time extremely gentle. His insatiable curiosity would encourage me to vigorously investigate the things that interested me. He also taught me that I may not be able to do a task perfectly, but for success, all I had to do was my best. As I taught my children I remembered those lessons. I know my dad would be happy to see them today and happy to see what they have become. I know they too will share with their children all they have learned that is best in fatherhood. I believe that they have all that they need to be good mentors, good leaders, and good examples.

The Son
Taking care of business, dogs and hot dogs...

When I was five years old, I remember my dad being out of work. Normally that would be a stressful situation, but looking back, I never remember him as anything but happy. He used the opportunity to take my brother and me to construction sites where he received permission to pick up steel and copper that were left over. We took the metal to the scrap yard.

"Pick it up boys, let's see how much we can get for it!"

We both took the task seriously and we felt like we were

doing something great with our dad. We stacked it up in our pick up and headed for the scrap yard. Once there we unloaded our treasure in two separate bins so it could be weighed. We waited in the truck. Our father came out of the office smiling with cash in his hand.

"OK, let's go for hot dogs!" he beamed.

"These are the best hot dogs I have ever had, Dad!" I informed him with delight as my brother and I wolfed down two large franks, the reward for our day of work and finding enough scrap metal to deserve it. I could see my father was pleased that we were happy. The hot dogs my father bought us were always the best! Even today, I rate hot dogs on the "Dad scale."

"Is this going to be your new job, Dad?" I asked in expectation.

"Well, we did make a bit today, but I doubt we would do as well on a regular basis!" he assured us.

I never gave that possibility much thought. Dad was always working and what he did next or how he provided for us was never a concern before. This was the first time I had any doubt.

"What will you do tomorrow then?" I wondered.

"Now, there is a concern you will not have to worry about. I already have something in the works."

"Something in the works" was a hallmark of my father. He never had an idle moment. Something was always on the burner, usually the front burner. His assurance put me at ease.

"Will we be able to look for metal again and get hot dogs, Dad?" I pleaded.

"Sure," he said, "it will be at least a monthly project for us!"

Back in the car I felt safe with him. He always knew the way to go and we always arrived where we were going. I looked at my brother and smiled. He had mustard on his chin and a smile on his face.

Dad made the best out of the worst. We did not have much, but as long as he was there, we never felt poor. My childhood was always an adventure. He would take us on that adventure and then we were allowed to sort it all out.

I remember that I was just out of kindergarten and it was time for vacation. I knew, from previous experience at our house, this could be a great time of adventure. The street we lived on was a dirt road and houses were being built down that road and all around us. It promised to be a time of discovery! I decided that Saturday morning after breakfast to head out to check out the machines and the new buildings that were being constructed. As I came closer to the first machine I could see that one of the workmen was still there. I was disappointed. I would not be able to have an adventure today. But wait! I could not believe it. Up there on that first machine, it was my dad, with his great big smile!

"What took you so long," he laughed. "Come on up on the other seat!"

I will never forget that first day of vacation. He spent the whole morning with me, showing me all the equipment, explaining what it did. We looked at the houses being constructed; he talked about how all that was done. Dad was there for me, enjoying the adventure with me. That's the kind of father I want to be for my children because I know how good that feels.

I recall a Christmas time when I was young. I came home in the afternoon, and entered the house to hear my mother's voice: "Close that door, it is freezing out there," she called to me from the kitchen.

"Where's Dad?" I asked her as my nose inspected the contents of our refrigerator.

"He's downstairs setting up the tree and could use some help! she answered.

Dad was excited about Christmas. Things were always tight in those days, but I can never remember that it mattered as we abounded in family customs and traditions and we always seemed to make so much out of the little we had.

"Ok Mom, I'll give him a hand," I said, munching on a stalk of celery I had taken from the crisper.

There was Dad, sitting on the floor, lotus position, separating the branches of our artificial tree into the proper size by colored tips with that same smile on his face. Our dog was right there also, sitting beside him, wondering why he thought this was so much fun.

"How come you are starting so early with the tree Dad?" I said, breaking his attention.

"Three more weeks to go until Christmas. This is part one," he responded without even looking up.

Part one it was indeed. He could make this the best time for us, inside and outside the house with those little things that would make our wishes come true.

I'll never forget the GI Joe Motor Home I wanted so much. It was certainly way beyond his budget, but he purchased it somehow. He secretly assembled the whole thing and it appeared on the floor Christmas morning. We had no idea of the whole story, and did not find out until two years later. When he assembled the Home, two oars were missing from the boat. On Christmas Eve, my father was up all night carving those oars himself, so that his son would not be disappointed that the gift was not complete. Dad believed that what you do is done for others. I know that I believe that too. That is what I would do for my daughter today.

I picked up my nine year old daughter this morning from

her mother's house. From that statement the reader has probably easily figured out my situation. I have not been as fortunate in marriage as my parents. It is nothing that I would have planned or would have ever thought would have occurred. In spite of it all, I will not let my daughter face any lack of parental love. I will do my best for her. Unlike many such arrangements in our society, this dad has custody. It is an awesome responsibility that I love and it gives purpose to my life. It is not an easy task, but I not only have the support of my parents, but also their example.

"C'mon, jump in, we have things to do!" I proudly announced as she slid in the front seat with her puppy in her arms.

"I think you should rename that dog," I tried to convince her.

"Ah, Dad, no way," she defiantly whined.

Somehow I did not think naming a dog "Business" was either good or appropriate. "Business" was first choice in the recent litter of my dad's dog and when she saw him she had instantly fallen in love. My mother had said something about taking that dog outside for his "business," and the name just stuck, at least in my daughter's mind. Mom just laughed and made some cute comment about it being "none of her business."

I think I am going to lose the battle on renaming Business. I can tell by the way she kisses him and holds him tight. Maybe I am a little jealous. Imagine that, competing with a dog for my daughter's affection!

"Daddy, can we get one of those new foot longs for lunch," she asked.

"You hungry now?" I wondered. When wasn't she hungry?

"Yes, I wasn't really hungry for much breakfast. Mom drank that milkshake stuff," she told me, making a wincing expression.

"Ok, we can go over there early for lunch. But you are going to have to leave Business in the car," I informed her.

I smirked at the thought of her exchanging one hot dog for another and a hot dog he would be if we did not leave the windows open!

"We can't take too long. It is not a wise idea to leave him in the car even with the windows open on a summer day," I warned her.

She seemed to understand the logic and encouraged Business into the back seat where he looked at her with doggy sadness.

"We'll be right back, Business," she cheerfully told him, as he twisted his head in disbelief.

We chose a table in the restaurant by the window with a view of the car. Business had his face against the car window watching the proceedings. I went up to the counter and ordered two foot longs, waited for the order and then picked up the condiments. I was heading back to the table when I heard the scream.

"No, Business, no! Stay there, stay there!"

As soon as she said it, she was out the door, her wails trailing behind her.

Dropping the foot longs at the nearest table I rushed to follow her out the door. I heard a pick-up screech to a halt and I was terrified at what greeted me outside. With sickening shock I found my daughter motionless against the front wheels of a truck. The driver had already jumped out of the cab, frantically trying to assist her. Somehow I screamed her name with all the energy and power which God had given me. Her back was humped up almost like she was kneeling in a fetal position, her arms pressed close to her body.

"Don't move her," I shouted at the driver as I arrived upon that sad scene. But I could see to my relief that she was moving herself, or at least she seemed to be. There was motion, first her arms, and then she seemed to sway back and forth. She moaned and with resolve she turned to expose to us the real cause of the movements. Sure enough it was Business, that she was protecting from those wheels, even before she protected herself.

"Don't be scared, Dad, Business is Ok," she cheerfully told me. "Where are the foot longs?"

She was Ok, Business was Ok, and the hot dogs were never better than on that morning. It was a great drive home too. The naming of Business seemed to have been resolved.

My father had taught me something that was more important than looking for someone to blame, or blaming myself. I have grown up not being afraid to be myself. My dad was not afraid and my daughter will not be afraid either. Whenever there is a crisis, hold on tight to the love you have. When you have little, make a big fuss over the little you have and revel in the gift you have been given. When you have nothing, seek out what is out there to be found and celebrate when you find it. It is a time of joy, and hot dogs. It is the time to be a rich man, a wise man, a father.

Following In My Father's Steps...

The preceding twenty stories were individually compiled from data provided from twenty interviews. It was not the intention to make the text purely biographical. Themes emerged as these men's words were reflected upon. It might be beneficial to reiterate those themes here, and to clarify for the reader the critical aspects of the father and son relationship as presented by the participants.

Some points that come from these stories indicate that:

✓ Sons want a relationship with their fathers.

✓ Sons want to understand their father in his story and in his work.

✓ Sons do not expect to have perfect fathers.

✓ Fathers often do not communicate with their sons.

✓ Fathers who are often absent can still be supportive and loving to a son.

✓ Fathers can connect with their sons in a shared activity.

✓ Sons need a father who will support them in times of change and growth.

✓ Sons benefit from a father who is focused.

✓ Sons take the expectations of their fathers seriously.

✓ Fathers can lead the way in helping sons understand relationships.

✓ Fathers remain as a safety assurance for their sons.

✓ Fathers and sons can both be role models and heroes.

Other themes may be found as the stories are read for a second time. Fathers and sons do well to reflect upon their relationships, to work to heal the lives that have been broken, and try to find a history that has never been told. Hopefully, these twenty stories might be a catalyst that start the repair of a relationship, initiate a story that has never been heard before, or open a door through which father and son enter into a new peace about their relationship. If any of those results can happen in the lives of fathers and sons, these life experiences were well worth printing.

FUTURE BOOKS ABOUT MY FATHER...

In My Father's Footprints
Authors: William Turner, Don Tapping
A book written about fatherhood from the perspective of the Baby Boomer.

This book will be a study of men in their middle age years, as they reflect upon their expectations in the past, their hopes for their children today, and their concerns about the future. The reader will note a sense of belonging that exists within the father and son relationship. As these fathers tell their stories, their hopes for the future may assist us in understanding our own fathers and sons, and help us to realize that our own stories can reach a positive conclusion.

In My Father's Path
Authors: William Turner, Don Tapping
A book written as senior fathers reflect upon their lives.

Fathers in their senior years look back upon their experiences with a distinct philosophical approach to the father and son relationship. A more spiritual emphasis has entered into their stories as they bring to conclusion such concerns from their early years as heard in *In my Father's steps*, and the mid-life reflections related in *In my Father's footprints*. Their stories and dialogue help readers to understand not only the lives of these men, and how they have come to a spirit of peace, but also encourage all fathers, as they advance in years, to understand the true value of their fatherhood and sonship.